Monetarist Economics

IEA Masters of Modern Economics
Series editor: Cento Veljanovski

Monetarist Economics

Milton Friedman

Basil Blackwell

Copyright © Institute of Economic Affairs 1991

First published 1991

Basil Blackwell Ltd
108 Cowley Road, Oxford, OX4 1JF, UK

Basil Blackwell, Inc.
3 Cambridge Center
Cambridge, Massachusetts 02142, USA

British Library Cataloguing in Publication Data

A CIP catalogue record for this book is available from the British Library.

Library of Congress Cataloging in Publication Data

Friedman, Milton, 1912–
    Monetarist economics/Milton Friedman.
        p.   cm.—(IEA masters of modern economics)
    Includes bibliographical references.
    ISBN 0–631–17111–8
    1. Chicago school of economics.   2. Monetary policy.   I. Title.
II. Series.
HB98.3.F74   1990
330.1—dc20   89–78251   CIP

Typeset in $10\frac{1}{2}$ on 12 pt Sabon by Butler & Tanner Ltd, Frome and London
Printed and bound in Great Britain by Butler & Tanner Ltd, Frome and London

Contents

Introduction

To most of us, Milton Friedman is instantly recognised as the great exponent of monetarism – the doctrine that 'money matters' – and probably the economist who has had more influence on government policies than any other economist since Lord Keynes. This popular perception, although correct, does, however, scant justice to Friedman's astonishingly wide range of contributions to knowledge and scholarship.[1]

Friedman's first major contributions to knowledge were in the field of mathematical statistics. In 1937 Friedman produced one of the seminal papers on analysis of variance of ranked data and was a pioneer of the new field of non-parametric methods. In the years of World War II, Friedman, working on the most practical problems in the statistical research group, virtually invented, in co-operation with Allen Wallis, a new field of statistics – sequential analysis. The new methods used sample information much more economically and enabled greatly improved systems of quality control to be employed in producing war material during the latter stages of World War II. (And – you guessed it – they were applied imaginatively and extensively in Japanese industry from the 1950s.) The main feature of these statistical contributions was not the formal analysis, which he often left to others, but the leaping imagination combined with a firm grasp of fundamentals.

Impressive as these contributions to statistical theory were, they remained, so to speak, only the by-product of his interests in empirical economics. He believed that economics should be regarded as a scientific discipline where tentative hypotheses are tested by comparing the predictions of the theory with actual outcomes. Theory was merely a way of rearranging one's assumptions and their logical implications. Only when it is shown that these implications are not inconsistent with evidence does the theory acquire substantive content and credibility.

The apotheosis of this approach was *A Theory of the Consumption Function* (Princeton, 1957) – a book which, I believe, virtually all academic economists would consider his most important work. The theory was simple: consumer spending is determined by one's wealth or permanent income, and will be largely unaffected by transitory receipts. This simplicity was matched by the most sophisticated elucidation of the implications and by an incomparable amassing, organisation, and interpretation of the evidence. His scholarly integrity was displayed by the diligent search for statistical and other evidence that could discredit his 'permanent income' hypothesis. Methodologically this book gave us a new standard for applied economics; clearly this is how it *should* be done. The predictive power of the theory was soon demonstrated when, in 1966–8 President Johnson, following impeccable Keynesian advice, tried to cool the overheating economy by a *temporary* tax increase: the Friedman hypothesis implied that Johnson would be disappointed – and he was. Fine fiscal tuning suffered but did not swiftly succumb. Governments still thought that they could trade off unemployment and inflation.

In December 1968, however, Friedman demonstrated that such a trade-off (the Phillips curve) was merely a short-run phenomenon. Attempts to pursue rates of unemployment below the 'natural rate' by expansionary fiscal and monetary policy would result in only transitory improvements in employment, but it will give rise to ever-accelerating inflation. The main lesson was that if governments target *real* variables, such as low unemployment and high rates of growth of output as an objective of macro-policy, then the outcome will be, on the one hand, disappointing growth and levels of unemployment and, on the other, escalating inflation.[2] Friedman convincingly explained the hitherto mysterious combination of recession and inflation ('stagflation') that afflicted all countries, particularly in the 1970s and 1980s.

Friedman's interest in monetary policy (illustrated here, in Readings 14, and in his *Memorandum on Monetary Policy*[3]) is based on a profusion of scholarship which, in our day, is matched only by that of Hayek. From the inauguration of the Chicago monetary workshop in 1951, Friedman and his students sought not merely to develop and manipulate monetary theory, but above all to test it critically against evidence in any country and epoque. The *Monetary History of the United States 1867–1960* (1963), written jointly with Anna Schwartz, amassed and analysed the evidence with a thoroughness and imagination never equalled in this field. The general results can be stated succinctly:

1   In the *long run*, nominal variations (in money) have only nominal

effects (on prices) and no real effects (on output and employment).

2   In the *short run*, variations in money have effects on real output and employment with highly variable lags, but such effects do not persist.

In essence, Friedman found that we could be fairly certain of the long-run equilibrium effects of monetary growth, but the dynamics of the short-run adjustments were much more shrouded in mystery and subject to forces, such as expectations and confidence, about which we know little.

The *Monetary History* provided a firm basis for Friedman's long-held view that the best monetary policy is one that increases the money supply at a constant but low rate, year in, year out. This will maintain a tolerable low rate of inflation and, at the same time, it will eliminate the avoidable oscillations in output and employment caused by variations in the monetary growth rate. Because it recognises our abiding ignorance of the dynamic process of short-term adjustment, it is humble in its claims: best to do no harm in the short run and provide for stable prices in the long run; best that the people know that monetary policy will conform to this simple rule, rather than be subject to the whims and wheezes of the authorities.

Although Friedman may properly complain about much that has been done under the banner of 'monetarism', virtually all countries of the West have at least embraced the principle of targeting a slow rate of monetary growth as their main plank in their attempt to contain inflation. Fine tuning has not disappeared but it has become a secondary and somewhat discredited gimmick. I believe that most of this change is due to Friedman, although he claims[4] that it was largely events, and particularly the inflations of the 1970s, which turned the tide. Friedman recognised that it would take some time to bring inflation under control and so he suggested adopting policies that would reduce some of the corrosive effects. The papers on indexation in this volume[5] suggest ways of house-training the beast of inflation. Although these practical (and widely adopted) policies are impeccably argued, I suspect that, among all his many policy proposals, most of us would have reservations about training the beast to become a pet. Pets can still be pests. It would be interesting to know what Friedman thinks after the experience of the last 15 years.

Notwithstanding this impressive record in monetary economics, perhaps most professional economists would regard Friedman's real forte as applied price theory. (We have but a soupçon in his paper, 'Roofs or Ceilings? The Current Housing Problem', on rent control.)[6]

Friedman's ability to simplify and distill the essence of a complex problem, and then to dazzle his readers or audience with his mastery of implications and evidence gives one some idea of the opportunity cost of his spending so many decades on monetary economics.

The cost is the greater, at least to those of liberal persuasions, because, along with Hayek, Friedman is one of the great champions of freedom. All his policy proposals are embedded in a framework of the rule of law and the promotion of individual liberties under that law. He has asserted his belief in the moral as well as the material superiority of a free society over a regulated and planned system.[7] After more than half a century of scholarly inquiry, the idea of a free society is making startling progress in countries which have long endured the repression of totalitarianism. I am sure Friedman would argue that ultimately good ideas triumph after we have experienced the consequences of bad ideas. True, but surely outstanding individuals such as Adam Smith and Milton Friedman make a great contribution. They do change history.

Sir Alan Walters

Notes

1   For a more extensive account of Friedman, see *Milton Friedman* entry in the *New Palgrave: A Dictionary of Economics*, John Eatwell, Murray Milgate and Peter Newman (eds), Macmillan, London, 1987.
2   See below; chapters 4 and 5.
3   See below; chapters 2 and 6.
4   In chapter 4 below.
5   See below, chapters 5 and 6.
6   Reproduced here as chapter 8.
7   See chapter 7 below.

1

The Counter-Revolution in Monetary Theory[1]

It is a great pleasure to be with you today, partly because I am honoured at being the first of the Harold Wincott lecturers, partly because economics owes so much to the work that has been done on this island. Coming back to Britain, as I am fortunate enough to be able to do from time to time, always means coming back to a warm circle of friends or friendly enemies.

I am going to talk this afternoon primarily about a scientific development that has little ideological or political content. This development nonetheless has great relevance to governmental policy because it bears on the likely effects of particular kinds of governmental policy regardless of what party conducts the policy and for what purpose.

A counter-revolution must be preceded by two stages: an initial position from which there was a revolution, and the revolution. In order to set the stage, I would like first to make a few remarks about the initial position and the revolution.

It is convenient to have names to describe these positions. The initial position I shall call the quantity theory of money and associate it largely with the name of an American economist, Irving Fisher, although it is a doctrine to which many prominent English economists also made contributions. The revolution, as you all know, was made by Keynes in the 1930s. Keynes himself was a quantity theorist, so that his revolution was from, as it were, within the governing body. Keynes's name is the obvious name to attach to the revolution. The counter-revolution also needs a name and perhaps the one most widely used in referring to it is 'the Chicago School'. More recently, however, it has been given a name

The First Wincott Lecture, delivered at the Senate House, University of London, 16 September 1970; published originally as IEA Occasional Paper No. 33 (1970).

which is less lovely but which has become so attached to it that I find it hard to avoid using it. The name is 'monetarism' because of the renewed emphasis on the rôle of the quantity of money.

A counter-revolution, whether in politics or in science, never restores the initial situation. It always produces a situation that has some similarity to the initial one but is also strongly influenced by the intervening revolution. That is certainly true of monetarism which has benefited much from Keynes's work. Indeed I may say, as have so many others since there is no way of contradicting it, that if Keynes were alive today he would no doubt be at the forefront of the counter-revolution. You must never judge a master by his disciples.

1 Irving Fisher and the Quantity Theory

Let me then start briefly to set the stage with the initial position, the quantity theory of money as developed primarily by Irving Fisher who is to my mind by far the greatest American economist. He was also an extraordinarily interesting and eccentric man. Indeed, I suspect that his professional reputation suffered during his life because he was not only an economist but also involved in many other activities, including being one of the leading members of the American prohibitionist party. He interviewed all potential presidential candidates for something like 30 years to find out what their position was on the subject of alcohol. His best-selling book, which has been translated into the largest number of languages, is not about economics at all but about health. It is about how to eat and keep healthy and is entitled *How to Live* (written jointly with Dr E. L. Fisk). But even that book is a tribute to his science. When he was a young man in his early thirties, he contracted tuberculosis, was given a year to live by his physicians, went out to the Far West where the air was good and proceeded to immerse himself in the study of health and methods of eating and so on. If we may judge the success of his scientific work by its results, he lived to the age of 80. As you may know, he was also a leading statistician, developed the theory of index numbers, worked in mathematics, economics, and utility theory and had time enough besides to invent the Kardex filing system, the familiar system in which one little envelope flaps on another, so you can pull out a flat drawer to see what is in it. He founded what is now Remington–Rand Corporation in order to produce and distribute his invention. As you can see, he was a man of very wide interests and ability.

$MV = PT$

The basic idea of the quantity theory, that there is a relation between the quantity of money on the one hand and prices on the other, is surely one of the oldest ideas in economics. It goes back thousands of years. But it is one thing to express this idea in general terms. It is another thing to introduce system into the relation between money on the one hand and prices and other magnitudes on the other. What Irving Fisher did was to analyse the relationship in far greater detail than had ever been done earlier. He developed and popularised what has come to be known as the quantity equation: $MV = PT$, money multiplied by velocity equals prices multiplied by the volume of transactions. This is an equation that every college student of economics used to have to learn, then for a time did not, and now, as the counter-revolution has progressed, must again learn. Fisher not only presented this equation, he also applied it in a variety of contexts. He once wrote a famous article interpreting the business cycle as the 'dance of the dollar', in which he argued that fluctuations in economic activity were primarily a reflection of changes in the quantity of money. Perhaps even more pertinent to the present day, he analysed in detail the relation between inflation on the one hand and interest rates on the other. His first book on this subject, *Appreciation and Interest*, published in 1896, can be read today with profit and is immediately applicable to today's conditions.

In that work, Fisher made a distinction which again is something that went out of favour and has now come back into common use, namely the distinction between the nominal interest rate in pounds per year per hundred pounds and the real interest rate, i.e. corrected for the effect of changing prices. If you lend someone £100 today and in 12 months receive back £106, and if in the meantime prices rise by 6 per cent then your £106 will be worth no more than your £100 today. The nominal interest rate is 6 per cent, but the real interest rate is zero. This distinction between the nominal interest rate and the real interest rate is of the utmost importance in understanding the effects of monetary policy as well as the behaviour of interest rates. Fisher also distinguished sharply between the actual real rate, the rate realised after the event, and the anticipated real rate that lenders expected to receive or borrowers expected to pay. No one would lend money at 6 per cent if he expected prices to rise by 6 per cent during the year. If he did lend at 6 per cent, it must have been because he expected prices to rise by less than 6 per cent: the realised real rate was less than the anticipated real rate. This distinction between the actual real rate and the anticipated real rate is of the greatest importance today in understanding the course of events. It explains why inflation is so stubborn once it has become imbedded, because as inflation accelerates, people come to expect it. They come to build the expected inflation into the interest rates that they are willing to pay as borrowers or that they demand as lenders.

Wide consensus

Up to, let us say, the year 1930, Irving Fisher's analysis was widely accepted. In monetary theory, that analysis was taken to mean that in the quantity equation $MV = PT$ the term for velocity could be regarded as highly stable, that it could be taken as determined independently of the other terms in the equation, and that as a result changes in the quantity of money would be reflected either in prices or in output. It was also widely taken for granted that short-term fluctuations in the economy reflected changes in the quantity of money, or in the terms and conditions under which credit was available. It was taken for granted that the trend of prices over any considerable period reflected the behaviour of the quantity of money over that period.

In economic policy, it was widely accepted that monetary policy was the primary instrument available for stabilising the economy. Moreover, it was accepted that monetary policy should be operated largely through a combination of two blades of a scissors, the one blade being what we in the USA call 'discount rate' and you in Britain call 'Bank rate', the other blade being open-market operations, the purchase and sale of government securities.

That was more or less the initial doctrinal position prior to the Keynesian revolution. It was a position that was widely shared. Keynes's *A Tract on Monetary Reform*,[2] which I believe remains to this day one of his best books, reflects the consensus just described.

2 The Keynesian Revolution

Then came the Keynesian revolution. What produced that revolution was the course of events. My colleague, George Stigler, in discussing the history of thought, has often argued that major changes within a discipline come from inside the discipline and are not produced by the impact of outside events. He may well be right in general. But in this particular instance I believe the basic source of the revolution and of the reaction against the quantity theory of money was a historical event, namely the great contraction or depression. In the United Kingdom, the contraction started in 1925 when Britain went back on gold at the pre-war parity and ended in 1931 when Britain went off gold. In the United States, the contraction started in 1929 and ended when the USA went off gold in early 1933. In both countries, economic conditions were depressed for years after the contraction itself had ended and an expansion had begun.

Wrong lessons from Great Depression

The Great Depression shattered the acceptance of the quantity theory of money because it was widely interpreted as demonstrating that monetary policy was ineffective, at least against a decline in business. All sorts of aphorisms were coined that are still with us, to indicate why it was that providing monetary ease would not necessarily lead to economic expansion, such as 'You can lead a horse to water but you can't make him drink' or 'Monetary policy is like a string: you can pull on it but you can't push on it', and doubtless there are many more.

As it happens, this interpretation of the depression was completely wrong. It turns out, as I shall point out more fully below, that on re-examination, the depression is a tragic testament to the effectiveness of monetary policy, not a demonstration of its impotence. But what mattered for the world of ideas was not what was true but what was believed to be true. And it was believed at the time that monetary policy had been tried and had been found wanting.

In part that view reflected the natural tendency for the monetary authorities to blame other forces for the terrible economic events that were occurring. The people who run monetary policy are human beings, even as you and I, and a common human characteristic is that if anything bad happens it is somebody else's fault. In the course of collaborating on a book on the monetary history of the United States, I had the dismal task of reading through 50 years of annual reports of the Federal Reserve Board. The only element that lightened that dreary task was the cyclical oscillation in the power attributed to monetary policy by the system. In good years the report would read 'Thanks to the excellent monetary policy of the Federal Reserve ...'. In bad years the report would read 'Despite the excellent policy of the Federal Reserve ...', and it would go on to point out that monetary policy really was, after all, very weak and other forces so much stronger.

The monetary authorities proclaimed that they were pursuing easy money policies when in fact they were not, and their protestations were largely accepted. Hence Keynes, along with many others, concluded that monetary policy had been tried and found wanting. In contrast to most others, he offered an alternative analysis to explain why the depression had occurred and to indicate a way of ameliorating the situation.

Keynes's critique of the quantity theory

Keynes did not deny Irving Fisher's quantity equation. What Keynes said was something different. He said that, while of course MV equals PT, velocity, instead of being highly stable, is highly adaptable. If the quantity of money goes up, he said, what will happen is simply that the velocity of circulation of money will go down and nothing will happen on the other side of the equation to either prices or output. Correspondingly, if something pushes the right-hand side of the equation, PT or income, up without an increase in the quantity of money, all that will happen will be that velocity will rise. In other words, he said, velocity is a will-of-the-wisp. It can move one way or the other in response to changes either in the quantity of money or in income. The quantity of money is therefore of minor importance. (Since I am trying to cover highly technical material very briefly, I am leaving out many qualifications that are required for a full understanding of either Fisher or Keynes. I do want to stress that the statements I am making are simplifications and are not to be taken as a full exposition of any of the theories.)

What matters, said Keynes, is not the quantity of money. What matters is the part of total spending which is independent of current income, what has come to be called autonomous spending and to be identified in practice largely with investment by business and expenditures by government.

Keynes thereby directed attention away from the rôle of money and its relation to the flow of income and toward the relation between two flows of income, that which corresponds to autonomous spending and that which corresponds to induced spending. Moreover, he said, in the modern world, prices are highly rigid while quantities can change readily. When for whatever reason autonomous spending changes, the resulting change in income will manifest itself primarily in output and only secondarily and only after long lags in prices. Prices are determined by costs consisting mostly of wages, and wages are determined by the accident of past history.

The great contraction, he said, was the result of a collapse of demand for investment which in turn reflected a collapse of productive opportunities to use capital. Thus the engine and the motor of the great contraction was a collapse of investment transformed into a collapse of income by the multiplier process.

The implications for policy

This doctrine had far-reaching implications for economic policy. It meant that monetary policy was of little importance. Its only rôle was to keep interest rates down, both to reduce the pressure on the government budget in paying interest on its debts, and also because it might have a tiny bit of stimulating effect on investment. From this implication of the doctrine came the cheap money policy which was tried in country after country following World War II.

A second implication of the doctrine was that the major reliance for economic stabilisation could not be on monetary policy, as the quantity theorists had thought, but must be on fiscal policy, that is, on varying the rate of government spending and taxing.

A third implication was that inflation is largely to be interpreted as a cost-push phenomenon. It follows, although Keynes himself did not draw this conclusion from his doctrine, that the way to counteract inflation is through an incomes policy. If costs determine prices and costs are historically determined, then the way to stop any rise in prices is to stop the rise in costs.

These views became widely accepted by economists at large both as theory and as implications for policy. It is hard now at this distance in time to recognise how widely they were accepted. Let me just give you one quotation which could be multiplied many-fold, to give you the flavour of the views at the end of World War II. Parenthetically, acceptance of these views continued until more recently in Britain than in the United States, so it may be easier for you to recognise the picture I have been painting than it would be now for people in the United States. I quote from John H. Williams, who was a Professor of Economics at Harvard University, a principal advisor to the Federal Reserve Bank of New York, and widely regarded as an anti-Keynesian. In 1945 he wrote: 'I have long believed that the quantity of money by itself has a permissive rather than a positive effect on prices and production.' And in the sentence I want to stress he wrote: 'I can see no prospect of a revival of general monetary control in the post-war period.' That was a very sweeping statement, and one that obviously proved very far indeed from the mark.

The high point in the United States of the application of Keynesian ideas to economic policy probably came with the new economists of the Kennedy administration. Their finest hour was the tax cut of 1964 which was premised entirely on the principles that I have been describing.

Having sketched briefly the initial stage of the quantity theory, and the revolutionary stage of the Keynesian theory, I come now to the monetarist counter-revolution.

3 The Counter-Revolution

As so often happens, just about the time that Keynes's ideas were being triumphant in practice, they were losing their hold on the minds of scholars in the academies. A number of factors contributed to a change of attitude towards the Keynesian doctrine. One was the experience immediately after World War II. On the basis of the Keynesian analysis, economists and others expected the war to be followed by another great depression. With our present experience of over two decades of inflation behind us it is hard to recognise that this was the sentiment of the times. But alike in the United States, in Great Britain and in many other countries, the dominant view was that, once World War II ended, once the pump-priming and government spending for military purposes ended, there would be an enormous economic collapse because of the scarcity of investment opportunities that had been given the blame for the Great Depression. Massive unemployment and massive deflation were the bugaboos of the time. As you all know, that did not happen. The problem after the war turned out to be inflation rather than deflation.

A second post-war experience that was important was the failure of cheap money policies. In Britain, Chancellor Dalton tried to follow the Keynesian policy of keeping interest rates very low. As you all know, he was unable to do so and had to give up. The same thing happened in the United States. The Federal Reserve System followed a policy of pegging bond prices, trying to keep interest rates down. It finally gave up in 1953 after the Treasury–Federal Reserve Accord of 1951 laid the ground-work for setting interest rates free. In country after country, wherever the cheap money policy was tried, it led to inflation and had to be abandoned. In no country was inflation contained until orthodox monetary policy was employed. Germany was one example in 1948; Italy shortly after; Britain and the United States later yet.

Reconsideration of Great Depression

Another important element that contributed to a questioning of the Keynesian doctrine was a re-examination of monetary history and particularly of the Great Depression. When the evidence was examined in detail it turned out that bad monetary policy had to be given a very large share of the blame. In the United States, there was a reduction in the quantity of money by a third from 1929 to 1933. This reduction in the quantity of money clearly made the depression much longer and more severe than it otherwise would have been. Moreover, and equally important, it turned out that the reduction in the quantity of money was not a consequence of the unwillingness of horses to drink. It was not a consequence of being unable to push on a string. It was a direct consequence of the policies followed by the Federal Reserve system.

From 1930 to 1933, a series of bank runs and bank failures were permitted to run their course because the Federal Reserve failed to provide liquidity for the banking system, which was one of the main functions the designers of the Federal Reserve system intended it to perform. Banks failed because the public at large, fearful for the safety of their deposits, tried to convert their deposits into currency. In a fractional reserve system, it is literally impossible for all depositors to do that unless there is some source of additional currency. The Federal Reserve system was established in 1913 in response to the banking panic of 1907 primarily to provide additional liquidity at a time of pressure on banks. In 1930–33, the system failed to do so, and it failed to do so despite the fact that there were many people in the system who were calling upon it to do so and who recognised that this was its correct function.

It was widely asserted at the time that the decline in the quantity of money was a consequence of the lack of willing borrowers. Perhaps the most decisive bit of evidence against that interpretation is that many banks failed because of a decline in the price of government securities. Indeed, it turned out that many banks that had made bad private loans came through much better than banks that had been cautious and had bought large amounts of Treasury and municipal securities for secondary liquidity. The reason was that there was a market for the government securities and hence when the bank examiners came around to check on the banks, they had to mark down the price of the governments to the market value. However, there was no market for bad loans, and therefore they were carried on the books at face value. As a result, many careful, conservative banks failed.

The quantity of money fell by a third and roughly a third of all banks failed. This is itself a fascinating story and one that I can only touch on. The important point for our purposes is that it is crystal clear that at all times during the contraction, the Federal Reserve had it within its power to prevent the decline in the quantity of money and to produce an increase. Monetary policy had not been tried and found wanting. It had not been tried. Or, alternatively, it had been tried perversely. It had been used to force an incredible deflation on the American economy and on the rest of the world. If Keynes – and this is the main reason why I said what I did at the beginning – if Keynes had known the facts about the Great Depression as we now know them, he could not have interpreted that episode as he did.

Wider evidence

Another scholarly element that contributed to a reaction against the Keynesian doctrine and to the emergence of the new doctrine was extensive empirical analysis of the relation between the quantity of money on the one hand, and income, prices and interest rates on the other. Perhaps the simplest way for me to suggest why this was relevant is to recall that an essential element of the Keynesian doctrine was the passivity of velocity. If money rose, velocity would decline. Empirically, however, it turns out that the movements of velocity tend to reinforce those of money instead of to offset them. When the quantity of money declined by a third from 1929 to 1933 in the United States, velocity declined also. When the quantity of money rises rapidly in almost any country, velocity also rises rapidly. Far from velocity offsetting the movements of the quantity of money, it reinforces them.

I cannot go into the whole body of scientific work that has been done. I can only say that there has arisen an extensive literature concerned with exploring these relations which has demonstrated very clearly the existence of a consistent relation between changes in the quantity of money and changes in other economic magnitudes of a very different kind from that which Keynes assumed to exist.

The final blow, at least in the United States, to the Keynesian orthodoxy was a number of dramatic episodes in our recent domestic experience. These episodes centred around two key issues. The first was whether the behaviour of the quantity of money or rates of interest is a better criterion to use in conducting monetary policy. You have had a curious combination in this area of central bankers harking back to the real bills doctrine of the early 19th century on the one hand, and Keynesians on the other, who alike agreed that the behaviour of interest rates was the relevant criterion for the conduct of monetary policy. By contrast, the new interpretation is that interest rates are a misleading index of policy and that central bankers should look rather at the quantity of money. The second key issue was the relative rôle of fiscal policy and of monetary policy. By fiscal policy, I mean changes in government spending and taxing, holding the quantity of money constant. By monetary policy, I mean changes in the quantity of money, holding government spending and taxing constant.

Fiscal versus monetary policy

The problem in discussing the relative rôles of fiscal policy and monetary policy is primarily to keep them separate, because in practice they operate jointly most of the time. Ordinarily if a government raises its spending without raising taxes, that is, if it incurs a deficit in order to be expansionary, it will finance some of the deficit by printing money. Conversely if it runs a surplus, it will use part of that surplus to retire money. But from an analytical point of view, and from the point of view of getting at the issue that concerns the counter-revolution, it is important to consider fiscal policy and monetary policy separately, to consider each operating by itself. The Keynesians regarded as a clear implication of their position the proposition that fiscal policy by itself is important in affecting the level of income, that a large deficit would have essentially the same expansionary influence on the economy whether it was financed by borrowing from the public or by printing money.

The 'monetarists' rejected this proposition and maintained that fiscal policy by itself is largely ineffective, that what matters is what happens to the quantity of money. Off-hand that seems like an utterly silly idea. It seems absurd to say that if the government increases its expenditures without increasing taxes, that may not by itself be expansionary. Such a policy obviously puts income into the hands of the people to whom the government pays out its expenditures without taking any extra funds out of the hands of the taxpayers. Is that not obviously expansionary or inflationary? Up to that point, yes, but that is only half the story. We have to ask where the government gets the extra funds it spends. If the government prints money to meet its bills, that is monetary policy and we are trying to look at fiscal policy by itself. If the government gets the funds by borrowing from the public, then those people who lend the funds to the government have less to spend or to lend to others. The effect of the higher government expenditures may simply be higher spending by government and those who receive government funds and lower spending by those who lend to government or by those to whom lenders would have loaned the money instead. To discover any net effect on total spending, one must go to a more sophisticated level – to differences in the behaviour of the two groups of people or to effects of government borrowing on interest rates. There is no first-order effect.

Evidence from the US 'experiments'

The critical first test on both these key issues came in the USA in 1966. There was fear of developing inflation and in the spring of 1966 the Federal Reserve Board, belatedly, stepped very hard on the brake. I say 'stepped very hard' because the record of the Federal Reserve over 50 years is that it has almost invariably acted too much too late. Almost always it has waited too long before acting and then acted too strongly. In 1966, the result was a combination of a very tight monetary policy, under which the quantity of money did not grow at all during the final nine months of the year, and a very expansive fiscal policy. So you had a nice experiment. Which was going to dominate? The tight money policy or the easy fiscal policy? The Keynesians in general argued that the easy fiscal policy was going to dominate and therefore predicted continued rapid expansion in 1967. The monetarists argued that monetary policy would dominate, and so it turned out. There was a definite slowing down in the rate of growth of economic activity in the first half of 1967, following the tight money policy of 1966. When, in early 1967, the Federal Reserve reversed its policy and started to print money like mad, about six or nine months later, after the usual lag, income recovered and a rapid expansion in economic activity followed. Quite clearly, monetary policy had dominated fiscal policy in that encounter.

A still more dramatic example came in 1968 and from 1968 to the present. In the summer of 1968, under the influence of the Council of Economic Advisers and at the recommendation of President Johnson, Congress enacted a surtax of 10 per cent on income. It was enacted in order to fight the inflation which was then accelerating. The believers in the Keynesian view were so persuaded of the potency of this weapon that they were afraid of 'overkill'. They thought the tax increase might be too much and might stop the economy in its tracks. They persuaded the Federal Reserve system, or I should rather say that the Federal Reserve system was of the same view. Unfortunately for the United States, but fortunately for scientific knowledge, the Federal Reserve accordingly decided that it had best offset the overkill effects of fiscal policy by expanding the quantity of money rapidly. Once again, we had a beautiful controlled experiment with fiscal policy extremely tight and monetary policy extremely easy. Once again, there was a contrast between two sets of predictions. The Keynesians or fiscalists argued that the surtax would produce a sharp slowdown in the first half of 1969 at the latest, while the monetarists argued that the rapid growth in the quantity of money would more than offset the fiscal effects, so that there would be a continued inflationary boom in the first half of 1969. Again, the monetarists proved correct. Then, in December 1968, the Federal Reserve Board did move to tighten money in the sense of slowing down the rate of growth of the quantity of money and that was followed after the appropriate interval by a slowdown in the economy. This test, I may say, is still in process, but up to now it again seems to be confirming the greater importance of the monetary than of the fiscal effect.

'This is where I came in'

One swallow does not make a summer. My own belief in the greater importance of monetary policy does not rest on these dramatic episodes. It rests on the experience of hundreds of years and of many countries. These episodes of the past few years illustrate that effect; they do not demonstrate it. Nonetheless, the public at large cannot be expected to follow the great masses of statistics. One dramatic episode is far more potent in influencing public opinion than a pile of well-digested, but less dramatic, episodes. The result in the USA at any rate has been a drastic shift in opinion, both professional and lay.

This shift, so far as I can detect, has been greater in the United States than in the United Kingdom. As a result, I have had in the UK the sensation that I am sure all of you have had in a continuous cinema when you come to the point where you say, 'Oh, this is where I came in.' The debate about monetary effects in Britain is pursuing the identical course that it pursued in the United States about five or so years ago. I am sure that the same thing must have happened in the 1930s. When the British economists wandered over to the farther shores among their less cultivated American brethren, bringing to them the message of Keynes, they must have felt, as I have felt coming to these shores in the opposite direction, that this was where they came in. I am sure they then encountered the same objections that they had encountered in Britain five years earlier. And so it is today. Criticism of the monetary doctrines in this country today is at the naïve, unsophisticated level we encountered in the USA about five or more years ago.

Thanks to the very able and active group of economists in this country who are currently working on the monetary statistics, and perhaps even more to the effect which the course of events will have, I suspect that the developments in this country will continue to imitate those in the United States. Not only in this area, but in other areas as well, I have had the experience of initially being in a small minority and have had the opportunity to observe the scenario that unfolds as an idea gains wider acceptance. There is a standard pattern. When anybody threatens an orthodox position, the first reaction is to ignore the interloper. The less said about him the better. But if he begins to win a hearing and gets annoying, the second reaction is to ridicule him, make fun of him as an extremist, a foolish fellow who has these silly ideas. After that stage passes the next, and the most important, stage is to put on his clothes. You adopt for your own his views, and then attribute to him a caricature of those views saying, 'He's an extremist, one of those fellows who says only money matters – everybody knows that sort. Of course money does matter, but . . . '.

4 Key Propositions of Monetarism

Let me finally describe the state to which the counter-revolution has come by listing systematically the central propositions of monetarism.

1 There is a consistent though not precise relation between the rate of growth of the quantity of money and the rate of growth of nominal income. (By nominal income, I mean income measured in pounds sterling or in dollars or in francs, not real income, income measured in real goods.) That is, whether the amount of money in existence is growing by 3 per cent a year, 5 per cent a year or 10 per cent a year will have a significant effect on how fast nominal income grows. If the quantity of money grows rapidly, so will nominal income; and conversely.

2 This relation is not obvious to the naked eye largely because it takes time for changes in monetary growth to affect income and how long it takes is itself variable. The rate of monetary growth today is not very closely related to the rate of income growth today. Today's income growth depends on what has been happening to money in the past. What happens to money today affects what is going to happen to income in the future.

3 On the average, a change in the rate of monetary growth produces a change in the rate of growth of nominal income about six to nine months later. This is an average that does not hold in every individual case. Sometimes the delay is longer, sometimes shorter. But I have been astounded at how regularly an average delay of six to nine months is found under widely different conditions. I have studied the data for Japan, for India, for Israel, for the United States. Some of our students have studied it for Canada and for a number of South American countries. Whichever country you take, you generally get a delay of around six to nine months. How clear-cut the evidence for the delay is depends on how much variation there is in the quantity of money. The Japanese data have been particularly valuable because the Bank of Japan was very obliging for some 15 years from 1948 to 1963 and produced very wide movements in the rate of change in the quantity of money. As a result, there is no ambiguity in dating when it reached the top and when it reached the bottom. Unfortunately for science, in 1963 they discovered monetarism and they started to increase the quantity of money at a fairly stable rate and now we are not able to get much more information from the Japanese experience.

4 The changed rate of growth of nominal income typically shows up first in output and hardly at all in prices. If the rate of monetary growth is reduced then about six to nine months later, the rate of growth of nominal income and also of physical output will decline. However, the rate of price rise will be affected very little. There will be downward pressure on prices only as a gap emerges between actual and potential output.

5 On the average, the effect on prices comes about six to nine months after the effect on income and output, so the total delay between a change in monetary growth and a change in the rate of inflation averages something like 12–18 months. That is why it is a long road to hoe to

stop an inflation that has been allowed to start. It cannot be stopped overnight.

6 Even after allowance for the delay in the effect of monetary growth, the relation is far from perfect. There's many a slip 'twixt the monetary change and the income change.

7 In the short run, which may be as much as five or ten years, monetary changes affect primarily output. Over decades, on the other hand, the rate of monetary growth affects primarily prices. What happens to output depends on real factors: the enterprise, ingenuity and industry of the people; the extent of thrift; the structure of industry and government; the relations among nations, and so on.

8 It follows from the propositions I have so far stated that *inflation is always and everywhere a monetary phenomenon* in the sense that it is and can be produced only by a more rapid increase in the quantity of money than in output. However, there are many different possible reasons for monetary growth, including gold discoveries, financing of government spending, and financing of private spending.

9 Government spending may or may not be inflationary. It clearly will be inflationary if it is financed by creating money, that is, by printing currency or creating bank deposits. If it is financed by taxes or by borrowing from the public, the main effect is that the government spends the funds instead of the taxpayer or instead of the lender or instead of the person who would otherwise have borrowed the funds. Fiscal policy is extremely important in determining what fraction of total national income is spent by government and who bears the burden of that expenditure. By itself, it is not important for inflation. (This is the proposition about fiscal and monetary policy that I discussed earlier.)

10 One of the most difficult things to explain in simple fashion is the way in which a change in the quantity of money affects income. Generally, the initial effect is not on income at all, but on the prices of existing assets, bonds, equities, houses, and other physical capital. This effect, the liquidity effect stressed by Keynes, is an effect on the balance-sheet, not on the income account. An increased rate of monetary growth, whether produced through open-market operations or in other ways, raises the amount of cash that people and businesses have relative to other assets. The holders of the now excess cash will try to adjust their

portfolios by buying other assets. But one man's spending is another man's receipts. All the people together cannot change the amount of cash all hold – only the monetary authorities can do that. However, as people *attempt* to change their cash balances, the effect spreads from one asset to another. This tends to raise the prices of assets and to reduce interest rates, which encourages spending to produce new assets and also encourages spending on current services rather than on purchasing existing assets. That is how the initial effect on balance-sheets gets translated into an effect on income and spending. The difference in this area between the monetarists and the Keynesians is not on the nature of the process, but on the range of assets considered. The Keynesians tend to concentrate on a narrow range of marketable assets and recorded interest rates. The monetarists insist that a far wider range of assets and of interest rates must be taken into account. They give importance to such assets as durable and even semi-durable consumer goods, structures and other real property. As a result, they regard the market interest rates stressed by the Keynesians as only a small part of the total spectrum of rates that are relevant.

11 One important feature of this mechanism is that a change in monetary growth affects interest rates in one direction at first but in the opposite direction later on. More rapid monetary growth at first tends to lower interest rates. But later on, as it raises spending and stimulates price inflation, it also produces a rise in the demand for loans which will tend to raise interest rates. In addition, rising prices introduce a discrepancy between real and nominal interest rates. That is why world-wide interest rates are highest in the countries that have had the most rapid rise in the quantity of money and also in prices – countries like Brazil, Chile, or Korea. In the opposite direction, a slower rate of monetary growth at first raises interest rates but later on, as it reduces spending and price inflation, lowers interest rates. That is why world-wide interest rates are lowest in countries that *have had* the slowest rate of growth in the quantity of money – countries like Switzerland and Germany. This two-edged relation between money and interest rates explains why monetarists insist that interest rates are a highly misleading guide to monetary policy. This is one respect in which the monetarist doctrines have already had a significant effect on US policy. The Federal Reserve in January 1970 shifted from primary reliance on 'money market conditions' (i.e. interest rates) as a criterion of policy to primary reliance on 'monetary aggregates' (i.e. the quantity of money). The relations between money and yields on assets (interest rates and stock market

earnings – price ratios) are even lower than between money and nominal income. Apparently, factors other than monetary growth play an extremely important part. Needless to say, we do not know in detail what they are, but that they are important we know from the many movements in interest rates and stock market prices which cannot readily be connected with movements in the quantity of money.

5 Concluding Cautions

These propositions clearly imply both that monetary policy is important and that the important feature of monetary policy is its effect on the quantity of money rather than on bank credit or total credit or interest rates. They also imply that wide swings in the rate of change of the quantity of money are destabilising and should be avoided. But beyond this, differing implications are drawn.

Some monetarists conclude that deliberate changes in the rate of monetary growth by the authorities can be useful to offset other forces making for instability, provided they are gradual and take into account the lags involved. They favour fine tuning, using changes in the quantity of money as the instrument of policy. Other monetarists, including myself, conclude that our present understanding of the relation between money, prices and output is so meagre, that there is so much leeway in these relations, that such discretionary changes do more harm than good. We believe that an automatic policy under which the quantity of money would grow at a steady rate – month in month out, year in year out – would provide a stable monetary framework for economic growth without itself being a source of instability and disturbance.

One of the most widespread misunderstandings of the monetarist position is the belief that this prescription of a stable rate of growth in the quantity of money derives from our confidence in a rigid connection between monetary change and economic change. The situation is quite the opposite. If I really believed in a precise, rigid, mechanical connection between money and income, if also I thought that I knew what it was and if I thought that the central bank shared that knowledge with me, which is an even larger 'if', I would then say that we should use the knowledge to offset other forces making for instability. However, I do not believe any of these 'ifs' to be true. On the average, there is a close relation between changes in the quantity of money and the subsequent course of national income. But economic policy must deal with the individual case, not the average. In any one case, there is much slippage. It is precisely this leeway, this looseness in the relation, this lack of a mechanical one-to-one correspondence between changes in money and in income that is the primary reason why I have long favoured for the USA a quasi-automatic monetary policy under which the quantity of money would grow at a steady rate of 4 or 5 per cent per year, month in month out. (The desirable rate of growth will differ from country to country depending on the trends in output and money-holding propensities.)

There is a great deal of evidence from the past of attempts by monetary authorities to do better. The verdict is very clear. The attempts by monetary authorities to do better have done far more harm than good. The actions by the monetary authorities have been an important source of instability. As I have already indicated, the actions of the US monetary authorities were responsible for the 1929–33 catastrophe. They were responsible equally for the recent acceleration of inflation in the USA. That is why I have been and remain strongly opposed to discretionary monetary policy – at least until such time as we demonstrably know enough to limit discretion by more sophisticated rules than the steady-rate-of-growth rule I have suggested. That is why I have come to stress the danger of assigning too much weight to monetary policy. Just as I believe that Keynes's disciples went further than he himself would have gone, so I think there is a danger that people who find that a few good predictions have been made by using monetary aggregates will try to carry that relationship further than it can go. Three years ago I wrote:

> We are in danger of assigning to monetary policy a larger rôle than it can perform, in danger of asking it to accomplish tasks that it cannot achieve and, as a result, in danger of preventing it from making the contribution that it is capable of making.[3]

A steady rate of monetary growth at a moderate level can provide a framework under which a country can have little inflation and much growth. It will not produce perfect stability; it will not produce heaven on earth; but it can make an important contribution to a stable economic society.

Notes

1   I chose this title because I used it about a dozen years ago for a talk at the London School of Economics. At that time, I was predicting. Now, I am reporting.
2   Macmillan, 1923.
3   Milton Friedman, 'The Role of Monetary Policy', Presidential Address to the American Economic Association, 29 December 1967; *American Economic Review*, March 1968 (reprinted in *The Optimum Quantity of Money and Other Essays*, Aldine, Chicago, 1969, pp. 95–110 – quotation from p. 99).

2

Monetary Correction

1 Synopsis

There is no technical problem about how to end inflation (section 2).
The real obstacles are political, not technical.

Ending inflation would deprive government of revenue it now obtains
without legislation (section 3). Replacing this revenue will require
government to reduce expenditures, raise explicit taxes, or borrow
additional sums from the public – all politically unattractive. I do not
know any way to avoid this obstacle.

Political obstacles to ending inflation

Ending inflation would also have the side-effect of producing a temporary, though perhaps fairly protracted, period of economic recession or
slowdown and of relatively high unemployment. The political will is
today lacking to accept that side-effect. Experience suggests that its
occurrence would instead produce an over-reaction involving accelerated
government spending and monetary growth that in its turn would
produce the initial side-effect of an unsustainable boom followed by
accelerated inflation. These side-effects of changes in the rate of inflation
arise because of the time it takes for the community to adjust itself to
changed rates of growth of spending. The time-delay distorts relative
prices, the structure of production and the level of employment. In turn,
it takes time to correct these distortions (section 4).

The side-effects of changes in the rate of inflation can be substantially

Published originally as IEA Occasional Paper No.41 (1974)

21

reduced by encouraging the widespread use of price escalator clauses in private and governmental contracts. Such arrangements involve deliberately eschewing some of the advantages of the use of money and hence are not good in and of themselves. They are simply a lesser evil than a badly managed money. The widespread use of escalator clauses would not by itself either increase or decrease the rate of inflation. But it would reduce the revenue that government acquires from inflation – which also means that government would have less incentive to inflate. More important, it would reduce the initial adverse side-effects on output and employment of effective measures to end inflation (section 5).

Legal enforcement

The use of escalator clauses in government contracts – taxation, borrowing, hiring, purchasing – should be required by law. Their use in private contracts should be permitted and enforceable at law but should be voluntary. The two are related because government adoption of escalator clauses, particularly in taxes, would remove serious impediments to their private adoption (section 6).

Objections to widespread escalation mostly reflect misconceptions about its effects. These misconceptions reflect the same confusion between relative prices and absolute prices that is responsible for many of the adverse effects of accelerated inflation or deflation and for misconceptions about the cause and cure of inflation (section 7).

2 The Technical Cause and Cure of Inflation

Short-run changes in both particular prices and in the general level of prices may have many sources. But long-continued inflation is always and everywhere a monetary phenomenon that arises from a more rapid expansion in the quantity of money than in total output[1] – though I hasten to add that the exact rate of inflation is not precisely or mechanically linked to the exact rate of monetary growth. (Figure 1 plots consumer prices in Britain and the ratio of the quantity of money to output over the last decade.)

This statement is only a first step towards an understanding of the causes of any particular inflation. It must be completed by an explanation of the reason for the rapid monetary growth. The rapid monetary growth

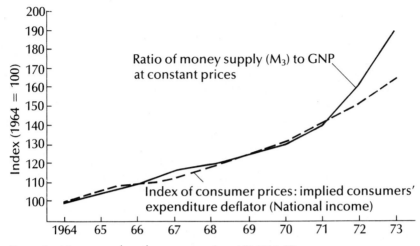

Figure 1   *Money supply and consumer prices: UK 1964–73.*
Note that the annual average money supply is lagged 6 months behind GNP (year ending June compared with GNP in calendar year).

that produced inflation in the USA from 1848 to 1860 reflected gold discoveries in California. The rapid monetary growth that produced world inflation from 1890 to 1914 reflected the perfection of the cyanide process for extracting gold from low-grade ore. The rapid monetary growth that has time and again produced wartime inflation has reflected the use of the printing press or its equivalent to finance wartime government spending.

Causes of world-wide growth of money supply

Under modern conditions, the quantity of money is determined by governmental monetary authorities. The accelerated increase in the quantity of money throughout the world in the past decade, which is responsible for the recent acceleration of inflation, has reflected a number of causes:

1   The attempt to maintain fixed exchange rates, which induced some

countries, notably Germany and Japan, to 'import' inflation from the USA.

2   The expansion in the rôle of government, and the reluctance to impose explicit taxes, which has induced many governments to use the implicit tax of inflation.

3   The commitment of governments to a policy of full employment, which has led them to over-react to temporary recessions by measures leading to rapid monetary growth.

Long-continued inflation can be ended only by a reduction in the rate of monetary growth. But, again, this statement is only a first step. The measures that can be used to reduce the rate of monetary growth may vary widely depending on the sources of the excess growth and the institutions of the country in question. For example, if monetary growth has reflected the financing of government expenditures by the printing press, it can be ended by (a) reducing government spending, (b) raising taxes, (c) financing the deficit in the government budget by borrowing from the public rather than by creating money. But method (c) may not be available for a country that does not have well-developed security markets. And all hyper-inflations have reflected governments so impotent and disorganised as to be unable to employ (b).

Importance – and limitations – of fiscal policy

As these comments imply, fiscal policy may play an important rôle in producing and curing inflation. Its influence is primarily through its effect on the quantity of money. But its influence can be offset by other forces affecting the quantity of money. Large government surpluses in the USA in 1919 and 1920 did not prevent rapid inflation because they were accompanied by rapid monetary growth which financed private spending. Large government deficits in the USA in 1931 to 1933 did not produce rapid inflation or prevent severe deflation because they were accompanied by a sharp decline in the quantity of money which sharply reduced private spending.

What matters for inflation is not simply the rate of monetary growth but the rate of growth relative to the rate of growth of output, and, in a more sophisticated presentation, relative to the rate of growth in the demand for real money balances at a constant level (or rate of change) of prices. This relationship has led many commentators to emphasise the rôle of 'productivity', arguing that inflation reflects a decline in productivity (or its rate of growth) and that a cure requires an increase in productivity (or its rate of growth). Though the rôle of output growth is, in principle, strictly symmetrical to the rôle of monetary growth, the quantitative orders of magnitude are wholly different. For any given country, over any period longer than a few years, the rate of output growth is unlikely to vary by more than a few percentage points – it would take a major structural change, for example, to raise the rate of growth of output in the USA by two percentage points, from, say, 3–4 per cent per year to 5–6 per cent.[2] On the other hand, the rate of monetary growth can and does vary over a much wider range – it can easily go from 3 or 4 per cent per year to 20 per cent per year. As a matter of experience, therefore, long-continued inflation is dominated by monetary changes rather than by changes in output.

The importance of the simple proposition in this section is that no measures are likely to produce long-continued inflation or to cure long-continued inflation unless they affect the long-term rate of monetary growth.

3 Government Revenue from Inflation

Since time immemorial, the major source of inflation has been the sovereign's attempt to acquire resources to wage war, to construct monuments, or for other purposes. Inflation has been irresistibly attractive to sovereigns because it is a hidden tax that at first appears painless or even pleasant, and, above all, because it is a tax that can be imposed without specific legislation. It is truly taxation without representation.

Three ways government gains from inflation

The revenue yield from inflation takes three major forms:

1 Additional government-created fiat money. Since ancient times, sovereigns have debased coinage by replacing silver or gold with base metals.[3] Later, paper currency supplemented token coins. More recently still, book entries at central banks (misleadingly called deposits) have been added. Governments use the fiat money that they issue to finance expenditures or repay debt. In addition, the fiat money serves as a base

on which the banking system creates additional money in the form of bank deposits.

In the calendar year 1973 the US government realised $8,000 million (£3,300 million) from this source – $6,000 million (£2,500 million) additional currency and coin in circulation on 31 December 1973 than on 31 December 1972, and more than $2,000 million (£830 million) in additional deposits at Federal Reserve Banks.[4]

2 Inflation increases the yield of the personal and corporate income tax by pushing individuals and corporations into higher income groups, generating artificial (paper) capital gains on which taxes must be paid, and rendering permitted depreciation allowances inadequate to replace capital, so taxing a return *of* capital to share-holders as if it were a return *on* capital. For the corporation tax alone, the US government realised in 1973 nearly $13,000 million (£5,420 million) from this source.[5]

3 The reduction in the real amount of outstanding National Debt. Much of this debt was issued at yields that did not allow for current rates of inflation. On a conservative estimate, the US government realised in 1973 something like $5,000 million (£2,000 million) from this source.[6]

All told, the US government's revenue from inflation totalled more than $25,000 million (£10,000 million) in 1973. Ending inflation would end this source of revenue. Government would have to reduce expenditures, increase explicit taxes, or borrow additional funds from the public at whatever interest rate would clear the market. None of these courses is politically attractive.

4 Side-Effects on Output and Employment

Acute appendicitis is accompanied by a high fever; the removal of the appendix will require that the patient stay in bed for some days. But the fever is not the cause of the appendicitis and bed-rest is not the cure. Both are side-effects.

The analogy with inflation is striking. The boom that typically accompanies the onset of accelerated inflation is not the cause of the inflation but a side-effect; the recession and unemployment that typically accompany the reduction of inflation are not the cure but a side-effect.

There are many ways to increase unemployment that would exacerbate inflation rather than cure it.

Time-lags lead to side-effects

Higher inflation reflects an acceleration in the growth rate of total money spending. Ending inflation requires a deceleration in the growth rate of total spending. The reason for the side-effects from such changes in total spending – both the boom which is generally regarded as a desirable side-effect and the recession which is uniformly regarded as an undesirable side-effect – is the time-delay between an increased or decreased rate of growth of total money spending and the full adjustment of output and prices to that changed rate of growth of total spending.

Essentially the same side-effects will arise whatever may be the cause of the changed growth rate in total spending – just as a high fever accompanies many different diseases and bed-rest many different cures. When non-monetary forces produce brief fluctuations in the rate of growth of total spending, the same side-effects occur. Also, if there is some cause other than unduly rapid monetary growth for long-continued inflation, or some cure other than reduced monetary growth, that cause and that cure will operate largely by affecting the growth rate in total money spending, and hence will produce much the same side-effects. Similarly, the measures proposed later to reduce the adverse side-effects of ending inflation will be effective whatever the cause and whatever the cure.

Hence the rest of this essay is relevant even if you do not accept my monetarist view as expressed in section 2.

Expectations slow to change

When total spending slows down, each producer separately tends to regard the reduction in the demand for his product as special to him, and to hope that it is temporary. He is inclined to meet it primarily by reducing output or accumulating stock, not by shading prices. Only after a time-lag will he start to shade prices. Similarly, any of his workers who are laid off are likely to react by waiting to be recalled or by seeking jobs elsewhere, not by moderating wage demands or expectations. A slowdown in total spending will therefore tend to be reflected initially in a widespread slowdown in output and employment and an increase in stocks. It will take some time before these responses lead in turn to widespread reductions in the rate of inflation and the rate of increase in wages. It will take still more time before *expectations* about inflation are revised and the revised expectations encourage a resumption of employment and output.

This is a highly simplified picture. Different activities have different time-speeds of adjustment. Some prices, wages, and production schedules are fixed a long time in advance; others can be adjusted promptly. As a result, a slowdown of total spending produces substantial shifts in *relative* prices, which will sooner or later have to be corrected; the correction in turn will cause economic disturbances.

For the USA, study of monetary history[7] indicates that the time-delay between a change in the rate of monetary growth and a corresponding change in the rate of growth of total spending and total output has averaged six to nine months; between the change in the rate of growth of spending and of prices, 12 to 18 months. Accordingly, the total delay between a change in monetary growth and in the rate of inflation has been about two years.[8] For the UK, the available evidence indicates that the time-delay is roughly the same as for the USA.

Serious effects on lending

The time-delay and resultant distortion are particularly clear for loans, where the distinction between *nominal* and *real* is especially important. Suppose you lend someone £100 in return for a promise to pay you £110 a year later. Neglect any possibility of default. What interest rate have you received? In pounds, 10 per cent. But if prices have risen by 10 per cent during the year, the £110 will buy only as much as the £100 would have done a year earlier. Your *real* return is nil. Indeed, if, as is true today, the £10 nominal return is subject to income tax, your *real* return is negative. You end up with *less* than you started with.

If you entered into a mortgage some years back, you may have paid 5 or 6 per cent. Given the inflation of the past few years, your effective *real* rate may have been nil. The rising price level probably raised the value of your property by as much as, or more than, the interest you paid. The lender in turn received a *real* return of nil – or a negative return if he was liable to tax. Similarly, consider someone who today takes out a mortgage at 11 per cent or more. Suppose economic policy were successful in bringing inflation down to nil. He would be in severe difficulties (unless of course the rate were reduced), and the lender would have received a wholly unexpected gain.

Failure of political will

Such side-effects constitute, I believe, the most important political obstacle to ending inflation, given, first, the commitment on the part of the US, UK and most other governments to 'full employment', secondly, the failure of the public at large to recognise the inevitable if temporary side-effects of ending inflation, and thirdly, the unwillingness or inability of political leaders to persuade the public to accept these side-effects.

Some years ago, when inflation was much lower than now, I believed that the re-adjustment required was sufficiently mild and brief to be politically feasible. But unfortunately in the USA the opportunity was cast aside on 15 August 1971, when President Nixon reversed economic policy by imposing a price and wage freeze and encouraging expansive monetary and fiscal policy. At the time, we were well on the way to ending inflation without severe side-effects. At the cost of the mild 1970 recession, the annual rate of inflation had been reduced from over 6 per cent to 4.5 per cent and was still declining. The economy was slowly recovering from that recession. Had the nation had the will – for President Nixon was reflecting a widespread national consensus when he reversed policy – another year of continued monetary restraint and of slow expansion would probably have turned the trick. As it was, the 1970 recession was a masochistic exercise rather than a side-effect of a successful cure.

Inflation in the USA is currently (mid-1974) far worse than in August 1971. The 14 per cent rate in the first quarter of 1974 was doubtless a temporary bubble, but, even on the most optimistic view, inflation is not likely to fall below 6 per cent during the coming year. Starting from that level, and with inflationary expectations even more deeply entrenched, an effective policy to end inflation would entail as a side-effect a considerably more severe and protracted recession than we experienced in 1970. The political will to accept such a recession, without reversing policy and re-stimulating inflation, is simply not present.

What then? If we – and probably Britain and other countries similarly placed – do nothing, we shall suffer even higher rates of inflation – not continuously, but in spurts as we over-react to temporary recessions. Sooner or later, the public will get fed up, will demand effective action, and we shall then have a really severe recession.

5 Easing the Side-Effects

How can we make it politically feasible to end inflation much sooner? As I see it, inflation can be ended sooner only by adopting measures that will reduce the side-effects from ending it. These side-effects fundamentally reflect distortions introduced into *relative* prices by *unanticipated* inflation or deflation, distortions that arise because contracts are entered into in terms of *nominal* prices under mistaken perceptions about the likely course of inflation.

Escalator clauses: an illustration

The way to reduce these side-effects is to make contracts in *real*, not nominal, terms. This can be done by the widespread use of escalator clauses.

Let me illustrate. In 1967 General Motors and the United Automobile Workers Union reached a wage agreement for a three-year period. At the time, prices had been relatively stable, consumer prices having risen at the average rate of 2.5 per cent in the preceding three years. The wage agreement was presumably based on an expectation by both General Motors and the union that prices would continue to rise at 2.5 per cent or less. That expectation was not realised. From 1967 to 1970, prices rose at an average annual rate of 5.2 per cent. The result was that General Motors paid *real* wages that were increasingly lower than the levels both parties had expected. The unexpected fall in real wages was a stimulus to General Motors, and no doubt led it to produce at a higher rate than otherwise. Initially, the unexpected fall in real wages was no deterrent to workers, since it took some time before they recognised that the accelerated rise in consumer prices was more than a transitory phenomenon. But by 1970 they were certainly aware that their real wages were less than they had bargained for.

The result was a strike in late 1970, settled by a wage agreement that provided: (1) a very large increase in the initial year; (2) much smaller increases for the next two years; and (3) a cost-of-living escalator clause.

The contract was widely characterised as 'inflationary'. It was no such thing. The large initial year increase simply made up for the effect of the past unanticipated inflation. It restored *real wages* to the levels at which both parties had expected them to be. The escalator clause was designed to prevent a future similar distortion, and it has done so.

This General Motors example illustrates a side-effect of unanticipated inflation. Suppose the same contract had been reached in 1967 but that the rate of inflation, instead of accelerating, had declined from 2.5 per cent to nil. Real wages would then have risen above the level both parties had anticipated; General Motors would have been driven to reduce output and employment; the workers would have welcomed the unexpectedly high real wage-rate but would have deplored the lower employment; when contract renewal was due, the union, not General Motors, would have been in a weak bargaining position.

An escalator clause which works both up and down would have prevented both the actual side-effects from unanticipated inflation and the hypothetical side-effects from unanticipated deflation. It would have enabled employers and employees to bargain in terms of the conditions of their own industry without having also to guess what was going to happen to prices in general, because both General Motors and the union would have been protected against either more rapid inflation or less rapid inflation.

Useful though they are, widespread escalator clauses are not a panacea. It is impossible to escalate *all* contracts (consider, for example, paper currency), and costly to escalate many. A powerful advantage of using money is precisely the ability to carry on transactions cheaply and efficiently, and universal escalator clauses reduce this advantage. Far better to have no inflation and no escalator clauses. But that alternative is not currently available.

Origins of the escalator: the 'tabular standard'

Let me note also that the widespread use of escalator clauses is not a new or untried idea. It dates back to at least 1707, when a Cambridge don, William Fleetwood, estimated the change in prices over a 600-year period in order to calculate comparable limits on outside income that college Fellows were permitted to receive. It was suggested explicitly in 1807 by an English writer on money, John Wheatley. It was spelled out in considerable detail and recommended enthusiastically in 1886 by the great English economist, Alfred Marshall.[9] The great American economist Irving Fisher not only favoured the 'tabular standard' – as the proposal for widespread indexation was labelled nearly two centuries ago – but also persuaded a manufacturing company that he helped to found to issue a purchasing-power security as long ago as 1925. Interest in the 'tabular standard' was the major factor accounting for the development of index numbers of prices. In recent years, the 'tabular standard' has been adopted by Brazil on a wider scale than I would recommend for the USA. It has been adopted on a smaller scale by Canada, Israel, and many other countries.[10]

6 The Specific Proposal

For the USA, my specific proposal has two parts, one for the Federal government, one for the rest of the economy. For the Federal government, I propose that escalator clauses be legislated; for the rest of the economy, that they be voluntary but that any legal obstacles be removed. The question of which index number to use in such escalator clauses is important but not critical. As Alfred Marshall said in 1886, 'A perfectly exact measure of purchasing power is not only unattainable, but even unthinkable.' For the USA, as a matter of convenience, I would use the cost-of-living index number calculated by the Bureau of Labor Statistics.

(a) The Government[11]

The US government has already adopted escalation for social security payments, retirement benefits to Federal employees, wages of many government employees, and perhaps some other items. Taxes which are expressed as fixed percentages of price or other value base are escalated automatically. The key additional requirement is for escalator clauses in the personal and corporate income tax and in government securities.

The personal tax. Minor details aside, four revisions are called for:
(i)   The personal exemption, the standard deduction, and the low income allowance should be expressed not as a given number of dollars, but as a given number of dollars multiplied by the ratio of a price index for the year in question to the index for the base year in which 'indexation' starts. For example, if in the first year prices rise by 10 per cent, then the present amounts should be multiplied by 110/100 or 1.10.
(ii)   The brackets in the tax tables should be adjusted similarly, so that, in the examples given, 0–$500 would become 0–$550, and so on. (These two measures have been adopted by Canada.)
(iii) The base for calculating capital gains should be multiplied by the

ratio of the price index in the year of sale to the price index in the year of purchase. This would prevent the taxing of non-existent, purely paper capital gains.

(iv)   The base for calculating depreciation on fixed capital assets should be adjusted in the same way as the base for calculating capital gains.

The corporate tax[12]

(i)   The present $25,000 (£10,400) dividing line between normal tax and surtax should be replaced by that sum multiplied by a price index number.

(ii)   The cost of stocks used in sales should be adjusted to eliminate book profits (or losses) resulting from changes in prices between initial purchase and final sale.

The base for calculating (iii) capital gains, and (iv) depreciation of fixed capital assets should be adjusted as for the personal tax.

Government securities[12] Except for short-term bills and notes, all government securities should be issued in purchasing-power form. (For example, Series E bonds should promise a redemption value equal to the product of the face value calculated at, say, 3 per cent per year and the ratio of the price index in the year of redemption to the price index in the year of purchase.) Coupon securities should carry coupons redeemable for the face amount multiplied by the relevant price ratio, and bear a maturity value equal to the face amount similarly multiplied by the relevant price ratio.

These changes in taxes and in borrowing would reduce both the incentive for government to resort to inflation and the side-effects of changes in the rate of inflation on the private economy. But they are called for also by elementary principles of ethics, justice, and representative government, which is why I propose making them permanent.

Taxation inflated to record levels   As a result largely of inflation produced by government in the USA, the UK and elsewhere, personal income taxes are today heavier than during the peak of Second World War financing, despite several 'reductions' in tax rates. Personal exemptions in real terms are at a record low level. The taxes levied on persons in different economic circumstances deviate widely from the taxes explicitly intended to apply to them. Government has been in the enviable position of imposing higher taxes while appearing to reduce taxes. The less enviable result has been a wholly arbitrary distribution of the higher taxes.

As for government borrowing, the savings bond campaigns of the US and UK Treasuries have been the largest bucket-shop operations ever engaged in.[13] This is not a recent development. In responding to a questionnaire of the Joint Economic Committee of Congress, I wrote as early as 1951:

> I strongly favour the issuance of a purchasing-power bond on two grounds: (a) It would provide a means for lower-and middle-income groups to protect their capital against the ravages of inflation. This group has almost no effective means of doing so now. It seems to me equitable and socially desirable that they should. (b) It would permit the Treasury to sell bonds without engaging in advertising and promotion that at best is highly misleading, at worst, close to being downright immoral. The Treasury urges people to buy bonds as a means of securing their future. Is the implicit promise one that it can make in good faith, in light of past experience of purchasers of such bonds who have seen their purchasing power eaten away by price rises? If it can be, there is no cost involved in making the promise explicit by adding a purchasing-power guarantee. If it cannot be, it seems to me intolerable that an agency of the public deliberately mislead the public.

Surely the experience of the nearly quarter-century since these words were written reinforces their pertinence. Essentially every purchaser of savings bonds or, indeed, almost any other long-term Treasury security during that period, has paid for the privilege of lending to the government: the supposed 'interest' he has received has not compensated for the decline in the purchasing power of the principal, and, to add insult to injury, he has had to pay tax on the paper interest. And the inflation which has sheared the innocent lambs has been produced by the government which benefits from the shearing.

It is a mystery to me – and a depressing commentary on either the understanding or the sense of social responsibility of business men (I say business *men*, not business) – that year after year eminent and honourable business leaders have been willing to aid and abet this bucket-shop operation by joining committees to promote the sale of US saving bonds or by providing facilities for payroll deductions for their employees who buy them.

(b) The private economy

Private use of escalator clauses is an expedient that has no permanent rôle, if government manages money responsibly. Hence I favour keeping private use voluntary in order to promote its self-destruction if that happy event arrives.

No legislation is required for the private adoption of escalator clauses, which are now widespread. Something over 5 million US workers[14] are covered by union contracts with automatic escalator clauses, and there must be many non-union workers who have similar implicit or explicit agreements with their employers. Many contracts for future delivery of products contain provisions for adjustment of the final selling price either for specific changes in costs or for general price changes. Many rental contracts for business premises are expressed as a percentage of gross or net receipts, which means that they have an implicit escalator clause. This is equally true for percentage royalty payments and for automobile insurance policies that pay the cost of repairing damage. Some insurance companies issue fire insurance policies the face value of which is automatically adjusted for inflation. No doubt there are many more examples of which I am ignorant.

It is highly desirable that escalator clauses should be incorporated in a far wider range of wage agreements, contracts for future delivery of products, and financial transactions involving borrowing and lending. The first two are entirely straightforward extensions of existing practices. The third is more novel.

'Indexation' for corporate loans   The arrangements suggested for government borrowing would apply equally to long-term borrowing by private enterprises. Instead of issuing a security promising to pay, say, interest of 9 per cent per year and to repay £1,000 at the end of five years, the XYZ company could promise to pay 3 per cent plus the rate of inflation each year and to repay £1,000 at the end of five years. Alternatively, it could promise to pay each year 3 per cent times the ratio of the price index in that year to the price index in the year the security was issued and to repay at the end of five years £1,000 times the corresponding price ratio for the fifth year. (The alternative methods are illustrated in table 1.) If there is inflation, the first method implicitly involves amortising part of the real value of the bond over the five-year period; the second involves currently paying interest only, at a constant real rate, and repaying the whole principal in *real* value at the end of the five years.

Table 1   *Hypothetical indexed bond: £1,000 five-year bond issued in 1968 at a real rate of 3 per cent*

Year	UK Consumer index (1968 = 100)	Price Level percentage change	Payments each year	
			Method 1 Interest(£)	Method 2 Interest(£)
1968	100			
1969	105.2	5.2	82	31.56
1970	112.0	6.5	95	33.60
1971	122.6	9.5	125	36.78
1972	131.0	6.8	98	39.60
1973	142.0	8.4	114	42.60
			Principal	
			£1,000	£1,420

So far, there has been little incentive for private borrowers to issue such securities. The delay in adjusting anticipations about inflation to the actual acceleration of inflation has meant that interest rates on long-term bonds have been extremely low in real terms. Almost all enterprises that have issued bonds in the past decade have done extremely well – the rate of inflation has often exceeded the interest rate they had to pay, making the real cost negative.

Lenders' changing expectations   Three factors could change this situation.

1   As lenders, who have been the losers so far, come to have more accurate expectations of inflation, borrowers will have to pay rates high enough to compensate for the actual inflation.
2   Government purchasing-power securities might prove so attractive that competition would force private enterprises to do the same.
3   Related to (2), if it became clear that there was a real possibility that government would follow effective policies to stem inflation, borrowing would no longer be a one-way street. Enterprises would become concerned that they might become locked into high-interest

rate loans. They might then have more interest in protecting themselves against inflation.

Businessmen's fears unwarranted   One question has invariably been raised when I have discussed this possibility with corporate executives: 'Is it not too risky for us to undertake an open-ended commitment? At least with fixed nominal rates we know what our obligations are.' This is a natural query from business men reared in an environment in which a roughly stable price level was taken for granted. But in a world of *varying* rates of inflation, the *fixed*-rate agreement is the more risky agreement. To quote Alfred Marshall again,

> Once it [the tabular standard] has become familiar none but gamblers would lend or borrow on any other terms, at all events for long periods.

The money receipts of most businesses vary with inflation. If inflation is high, their receipts in money terms are high and they can pay the escalated rate of interest; if inflation is low, their receipts are low and they will find it easier to pay the low rate with the adjustment for inflation than a fixed but high rate; and similarly at the time of redemption.

The crucial point is the relation between assets and liabilities. Currently, for many enterprises, their assets, including goodwill, are real in the sense that their money value will rise or fall with the general price level; but their liabilities tend to be nominal, i.e. fixed in money terms. Accordingly, these enterprises benefit from inflation at a higher rate than was anticipated when the nominal liabilities were acquired and are harmed by inflation at a lower rate than was anticipated. If assets and liabilities were to match, such enterprises would be protected against either event.

Home mortgages – threat of 'major crisis'   A related yet somewhat different case is provided by financial intermediaries. Consider savings and loan associations and mutual savings banks. Both their assets (primarily home mortgages) and their liabilities (due to shareholders or depositors) are expressed in money terms. But they differ in time duration. The liabilities are in practice due on demand;[15] the assets are long term. The current mortgages were mostly issued when inflation, and therefore interest rates, were much lower than they are now. If the mortgages were re-valued at current yields, i.e. at the market prices for which they could be sold in a free secondary market, every US savings and loan association would be technically insolvent.

So long as the thrift institutions can maintain their level of deposits, no problem arises because they do not have to liquidate their assets. But if inflation speeds up, interest rates on market instruments will rise further. Unless the thrift institutions offer competitive interest rates, their shareholders or depositors will withdraw funds to get a better yield (the process inelegantly termed 'disintermediation'). But with their income fixed, the thrift institutions will find it difficult or impossible to pay competitive rates. This situation is concealed but not altered by the legal limits on the rates they are permitted to pay.

Further acceleration of inflation threatens a major crisis for this group of financial institutions. And the crisis is no minor matter. Total assets of these US institutions approach $400,000 million (£167,000 million).[16] As it happens, they would be greatly helped by a deceleration of inflation, but some of their recent borrowers who are locked into high rates on mortgages would be seriously hurt.[17]

Benefits of inflation-proofed loans   Consider how different the situation of the thrift institutions would be with widespread escalator clauses: the mortgages on their books would be yielding, say, 5 per cent plus the rate of inflation; they could afford to pay to their shareholders or depositors, say, 3 or 4 per cent plus the rate of inflation. They, their borrowers, and their shareholders or depositors would be fully protected against changes in the rate of inflation. They would be assuming risks only with respect to the much smaller possible changes in the *real* rate of interest rather than in the money rate.

Similarly an insurance company could afford to offer an inflation-protected policy if its assets were in inflation-protected loans to business or in mortgages or government securities. A pension fund could offer inflation-protected pensions if it held inflation-protected assets. In Brazil, where this practice has, to my knowledge, been carried furthest, banks are required to credit a 'monetary correction' equal to the rate of inflation on all time deposits and to charge a 'monetary correction' on all loans extending beyond some minimum period.

To repeat, none of these arrangements is without cost. It would be far better if stable prices made them unnecessary. But they seem to me far less costly than continuing on the road to periodic acceleration of inflation, ending in a real bust.

The suggested governmental arrangements would stimulate the private arrangements. Today, one deterrent to issuing private purchasing-power securities is that the inflation adjustment would be taxable to the recipient along with the real interest paid. The proposed tax changes would in effect exempt such adjustments from taxation, and so make purchasing-power securities more attractive to lenders. In addition, government issues of purchasing-power securities would offer effective competition to private borrowers, inducing them to follow suit, and would provide assets that could be used as the counterpart of inflation-protected liabilities.

Prospects for private contract escalators   Would escalator clauses spread in private contracts? That depends on the course of inflation. If, by some miracle, inflation were to disappear in the near future, all talk of such arrangements would also disappear. The more likely development is that US inflation will taper off in late 1974, will settle at something like 6 or 7 per cent in 1975, and will then start to accelerate in 1976 in response to the delayed impact of over-reaction in 1974 to rising unemployment. During this period there will be a steady but unspectacular expansion of escalator clauses. If inflation accelerates to 10 per cent and beyond in 1977 or so, the steady expansion will turn into a bandwagon.

Needless to say, I hope this scenario is wrong. I hope that the Federal

CHART 1

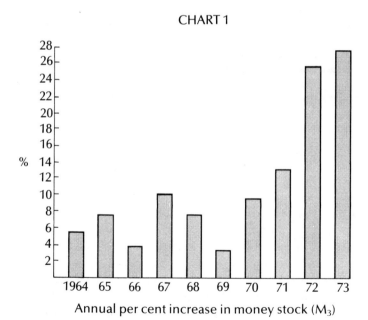

Annual per cent increase in money stock (M₃)

Money Supply, UK.

Reserve and the Administration will be willing and able to resist the pressure to over-react to the 1974 recession, that they will maintain fiscal and monetary restraint, and so avoid another acceleration of inflation. But neither past experience, nor the present political climate, makes that hope a reasonable expectation.

CHART 2

Annual Per cent Increase

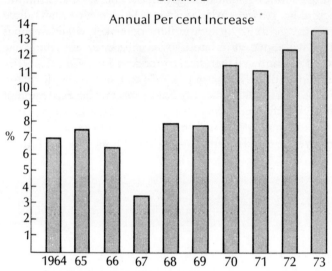

Weekly earnings in industry, UK.

Making it easier to fight inflation   How would widespread adoption of the escalator principle affect economic policy? Some critics say indexation would condemn us to perpetual inflation. I believe that, on the contrary, indexation would enhance government's ability to act against inflation.

To begin with, indexation will temper some of the hardships and distortions that now follow from a drop in the rate of inflation. Employers will not be stuck with excessively high wage increases under existing union contracts, for wage increases will moderate as inflation recedes. Borrowers will not be stuck with excessively high interest costs, for the rates on outstanding loans will moderate as inflation recedes. Indexation will also partly counteract the tendency of businesses to defer capital investment once total spending begins to decline – there will be less reason to wait in expectation of lower prices and lower interest rates. Businesses will be able to borrow funds or enter into construction contracts knowing that interest rates and contract prices will be adjusted later in accord with indexes of prices.

Most important, indexation will shorten the time it takes for a reduction in the rate of growth of total spending to have its full effect in reducing the rate of inflation. As the deceleration of demand pinches at various points in the economy, any effects on prices will be transmitted promptly to wage contracts, contracts for future delivery, and interest rates on outstanding long-term loans. Accordingly, producers' wage costs and other costs will go up less rapidly than they would without indexation. This tempering of costs, in turn, will encourage employers to keep more people on the payroll, and produce more goods, than they would without indexation. The encouragement of supply, in turn, will work against price increases, with additional moderating feedback on wages and other costs.

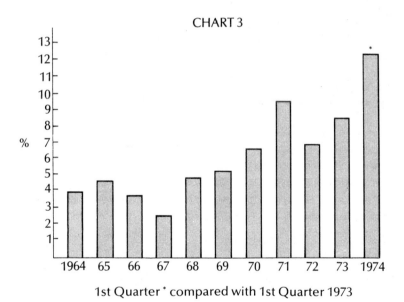

CHART 3

1st Quarter * compared with 1st Quarter 1973

Retail prices, UK

With widespread indexation, in sum, firm monetary restraint by the Federal Reserve System (the 'Fed') would be reflected in a much more even reduction in the pace of inflation and a much smaller transitory rise in unemployment. The success in slowing inflation would steel political will to suffer the smaller withdrawal pains and so might make it possible for the 'Fed' to persist in a firm policy. As it became credible that the 'Fed' would persist, private reactions could reinforce the effects of its policy. The economy would move to non-inflationary growth at high levels of employment much more rapidly than now seems possible.

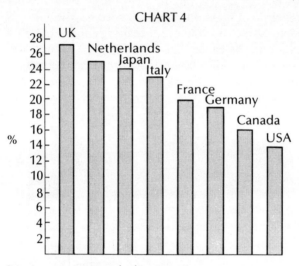

Price increase in UK and other countries.

7 Objections to Escalator Clauses

The major objection to widespread escalation is the allegation that escalators have an inflationary impact on the economy.[18] In this simple-minded form, the statement is simply false – as I noted earlier in connection with the 1970 General Motors settlement. An escalator goes into effect only as the *result* of a *previous* price increase. Whence came that? An escalator can go down as well as up. If inflation slows, and hence so do wage increases, do escalators have a *deflationary* impact?

In the first instance, escalators have *no* direct effect on the rate of inflation. They simply assure that inflation affects different prices and wages alike and thus avoid the kind of distortions in relative prices and wages illustrated by the General Motors case. With widespread escalation, inflation would be *transmitted* more quickly and evenly, and hence the harm done by inflation would be less. But why should that raise or lower the *rate* of inflation?

Incentive to raise tax rates?

Two objections have been made on a more sophisticated level. First, widespread escalation would restrict the government revenue from inflation simply to the direct tax on cash balances produced by the issue of additional high-powered money (point (1), p.25). It would thereby reduce the revenue from a given rate of inflation, which could induce government to raise the rate of tax.

'Living with inflation'

Second, the general public could interpret the adoption of escalator clauses as demonstrating that the government has given up the fight against inflation, and is seeking only to 'live with inflation'. This might lead the public to raise its own anticipations of future inflation, which, by reducing its willingness to hold cash balances, could cause a once-for-all rise in the price level and to that extent be a self-fulfilling prophecy.

Neither objection seems to me weighty. If the public does not wish to stop inflation but is content to allow government to use inflation as a regular source of revenue, the sooner we adapt our institutions to that situation the better. Similarly, the second objection has little relevance to the proposal for escalator clauses as a means for removing *political* obstacles to ending inflation.

On a still more sophisticated level, it can be argued that, by removing distortions in relative prices produced by inflation, widespread escalator clauses would make it easier for the public to recognise changes in the rate of inflation, would thereby reduce the time-lag in adapting to such changes, and thus make the nominal price level more sensitive and variable. This is certainly possible, though by no means demonstrated. But, if so, the *real variables* would be made *less* sensitive and *more* stable – a highly beneficial trade-off. Moreover, it is also possible that, by making accurate estimates of the rate of inflation less important, widespread escalator clauses would reduce the attention devoted to such estimates, and thereby provide more stability.

An objection of a very different kind is that inflation serves the critical social purpose of resolving incompatible demands by different groups. To put it crudely, the participants in the economy have 'non-negotiable demands' for more than the whole output. These demands are reconciled because inflation fools people into believing that their demands have been met when in fact they have not been, nominal returns being eroded by unanticipated inflation.

Escalator clauses, it is argued, bring the inconsistent demands into the open. Workers who would accept a lower real wage produced by unanticipated inflation will not be willing to accept the same real wage in explicit negotiations.[19] If this view is correct on a wide enough scale to be important, I see no ultimate outcome other than either runaway inflation or an authoritarian society ruled by force. Perhaps it is only wishful thinking that makes me reluctant to accept this vision of our fate.

8 Conclusion

The conventional political wisdom is that the citizenry may mutter about inflation but votes on the basis of the level of unemployment. Nobody, it is said, has ever lost an election because of inflation: Hoover in 1932 and Nixon in 1960 lost because of unemployment.

As we leave the depression decade farther and farther behind, and as we experience more and more inflation, this conventional wisdom becomes increasingly questionable. Inflation surely helped to make Mr Edward Heath Prime Minister in 1970 and, even more surely, ex-Prime Minister in 1974. The popularity of Japan's Prime Minister, Mr K. Tanaka, is at an all-time low because of inflation. President Allende of Chile lost his life at least partly because of inflation. Throughout the world, inflation is a major source of political unrest.

Perhaps widespread escalator clauses are not the best expedient in this time of trouble. But I know of no other that has been suggested that holds out as much promise of both reducing the harm done by inflation and facilitating the ending of inflation. If inflation continues to accelerate, the conventional political wisdom will be reversed. The insistence on ending inflation at whatever cost will lead to a severe depression. Now, before that has occurred, is the time to take measures that will make it politically feasible to end inflation before inflation ends not only the conventional wisdom but perhaps also the free society.

Notes

1   This is a bit of an over-simplification, because a fully defensible statement would have to allow for autonomous changes in velocity, i.e. in the demand for real balances, and would have to specify the precise definition of 'money'. But I know of no case in which these qualifications are of critical importance.

2   [In the UK the 1970–74 Conservative Government hoped to raise the annual rate of growth from 2.5–3 per cent in the late 1960s to 5 per cent. For a short period in 1972–73 it rose to $6\frac{1}{2}$ per cent (if the official measurements are reliable), but then fell to 4 per cent in 1973. – Ed.]

3   One historian of money describes the debasement of the Roman *denarius* from an initially full-bodied silver coin until, by the time of Emperor Diocletian (300 AD), it had become 'practically a copper coin being only slightly washed with silver'. (Rupert J. Ederer, *The Evolution of Money*, Public Affairs Press, Washington DC, 1964, p. 88.) We have gone further than Diocletian. We wash our copper coins now with nickel, so that not even a trace of silver remains.

4   Excluding Treasury deposits. Nominally, the Federal Reserve Banks are owned by their member banks. This a pure formality. In practice the Federal Reserve System is part of the government. It earns 'income' in the form of 'interest' paid to it by the US Treasury on government securities; it returns the excess of such 'interest' over operating expenses to the Treasury. Economic understanding is promoted and confusion avoided by consolidating the accounts of the Federal Reserve System with those of the Treasury.

5   Inflation produced an over-statement of 1973 corporate profits by more than $26,000 million (£10,800 million) through spurious profits on stocks and under-depreciation, according to Department of Commerce estimates summarised by George Terborgh, *Inflation and Profits*, Machinery and Allied Products Institute (revised, 2 April 1974). At a 48 per cent corporate tax rate, the additional tax paid was about $12,800 million (£5,300 million). In addition, corporate capital gains were undoubtedly over-stated.

6   Total interest paid on the roughly $260,000 million (£108,000 million) of Federal debt held by the public was at an average rate of about 5.7 per cent. A 1973 market rate would have been about two percentage points higher, which means that the revenue to the government on this basis was about

$5,000 million (£2,000 million). However, in retrospect, it seems clear that 1973 market rates did not adequately allow for inflation.

7   Milton Friedman, *The Optimum Quantity of Money*, Macmillan, London, 1969, chs 10, 11 and 12; 'Letter on Monetary Policy', *Review*, Federal Reserve Bank of Saint Louis, March 1974. Also, A. James Meigs, *Money Matters*, Harper and Row, New York, 1972, ch. 6.

8   This is precisely what W. Stanley Jevons estimated it to be: 'An expansion of the currency occurs one or two years prior to a rise of prices.' (*Investigations into Currency and Finance*, Macmillan, 1884, p. 107.)

9   His discussion is reproduced in a Note to the original *Occasional Paper*, at p. 33.

10   A useful survey is in Robert P. Collier, *Purchasing Power Bonds and Other Escalated Contracts*, Buffalo Book Co., Taipei, Taiwan, 1969 (distributed in the USA by the Utah State University Press, Logan, Utah).
     [The British Government began to review pensions and other social benefits annually in the light of rising prices in 1973 and the Conservative Party promised revision twice a year in its 1974 election manifesto. – ED.]

11   [In principle, with change of detail, these observations apply, or could apply, to Britain. Cf. the note on 'Fiscal Drag and Inflation' in the original *Occasional Paper*, at p. 49. ED.]

12   These tax and borrowing measures are all contained in a Bill introduced by Senator James Buckley in April 1974.

13   [In the UK the *Report* of the Committee to Review National Savings (the Page Committee: Cmnd. 5273, HMSO, June 1973) found that 'the £9,546 million of National Savings invested at the end of March 1972 was worth only £4,269 million if expressed in the purchasing power of money in March 1951. Since the total value of National Savings at end March 1951 was £6,130 million, in real terms National Savings are contracting' (para. 568). It therefore examined the arguments for and against index-linking for government securities and concluded that 'an experiment should be undertaken of issuing a modest index-linked bond for the small saver on the grounds that he is least able to protect his capital against inflation' (para. 583). – ED.]

14   [Eight to nine million in the UK where threshold agreements have been widely adopted since they received the Conservative Government's sanction in its counter-inflation policy: *The price and pay code for Stage 3. A consultative document*, Cmnd. 5444, HMSO, Autumn 1973. – ED.]

15   [Or, in Britain, at short notice. – ED.]

16   [British building society assets exceed £17,500 million. – ED.]

17   [Unless interest rates are lowered, as they would be in Britain. – ED.]

18   [A Treasury Minister in the 1970–74 Conservative Government has argued that those who advocate indexation are 'arguing that one ought to try to live with inflation rather than control it, which I regard as a dangerous point from which to start'. (Mr Terence Higgins, *Hansard*, 20 May 1974, col. 83.) – ED.]

19 [This is essentially the 'money illusion' behind Keynes's view that workers
    would not accept lower money wages but would accept lower real wages
    resulting from unchanged (or even rising) money wages reduced in real
    value by rising prices (inflation). – ED.]

3

Memorandum: Response to Questionnaire on Monetary Policy

1 The Background

1 Britain, like the US and many other countries, faces two different though related problems: inflation and slow growth. Though one word, 'stagflation', has been used to encompass both, the two problems are separable: Salazar's Portugal had no inflation and no growth; late 19th-century US and Britain, deflation and rapid growth; many countries in the 1930s, deflation and contraction; post-war Germany and Switzerland, low inflation and rapid growth; Brazil in the 1960s and early 1970s and Korea more recently, high inflation and rapid growth; Britain, the US and many other countries currently, high inflation and slow growth or contraction.

2 Inflation over any substantial period is always and everywhere a monetary phenomenon, arising from a more rapid growth in the quantity of money than in output. Few economic propositions are more firmly grounded in experience – extending over thousands of years and the face of the globe. But this proposition is the beginning of an understanding of the cause and cure of inflation, not the end. The hard questions are *why* the quantity of money expands more rapidly than output and *how* the difference can be eliminated. With respect to 'how', though inflation depends on both the rate of monetary growth and rate of output growth, a cure must operate primarily via monetary policy for two reasons, (1) Monetary growth, like inflation, can and does vary over a much wider range than output growth. Doubling the trend rate of output growth in

This memorandum was presented on 11 June 1980 to the Chairman of the Treasury and Civil Service Committee.

49

a few years would be phenomenal, yet for the UK, that would reduce inflation by only two or three percentage points. (2)Though a slower rate of inflation may have favourable effects on output growth after an interval, a temporary side-effect is almost certain to be slower output growth rather than the higher growth needed to counter inflation (see paragraph 5 below).

3 The retardation of growth in the UK and the US in recent years reflects primarily, in my opinion, an earlier explosion in government spending and government intervention into the economy, which has impaired incentives to work, save, invest, and innovate, and has fostered misuse of existing resources. Here, monetary policy is distinctly the junior partner in a cure; policies to remove obstacles to the effective use of resources, the senior partner.

4 The current problems of inflation and slow growth are related in several ways.

(a)   Both are largely the common consequences of the same basic cause: too big and too intrusive a government. Higher government spending provokes taxpayer resistance. Taxpayer resistance encourages government to finance spending by monetary creation, thereby increasing monetary growth and hence inflation, which, as a by-product very welcome to legislators, raises effective tax rates without legislation. Government spending plus government intervention reduce output growth, thereby further raising inflation for any given rate of monetary growth. Slower growth also increases the burden on the community of any given level of government spending, exacerbating the resistance to explicit taxation.

(b)   Inflation, particularly highly variable inflation, interferes with growth by (i) introducing static into the messages transmitted by the price system, increasing the uncertainty facing individuals and business enterprises, which encourages them to divert attention from productive to protective activities, and (ii) inducing governments to adopt such counterproductive false cures as price controls and incomes policies. As noted in paragraph 1, these adverse effects have sometimes been more than offset by other forces, so that high inflation has not prevented rapid growth. However, under current conditions in Western advanced countries, the adverse effects have been dominant during the past two decades: high and rising inflation has been accompanied by high and rising unemployment and by low and declining growth.

(c) Both inflation and slow growth have been made worse by the energy crisis. However, both problems preceded the energy crisis, some countries have managed to avoid both inflation and slow growth despite the energy crisis, and neither problem would be resolved if the crisis should miraculously end. In any event, for Britain the energy crisis, thanks to North Sea oil, has been a boon as well as a burden. The harm done by the energy crisis has been exacerbated, and its likely duration greatly extended, by mistaken policies adopted by many governments in response to the OPEC Cartel.

5 A successful policy of reducing inflation will have as an unavoidable side-effect a temporary retardation in economic growth. However, continuation of the present levels of inflation, and even more further acceleration of inflation would at best postpone the retardation at the expense of a more severe retardation later. Past mistakes in economic policy have left us with no soft options. Our only real alternatives are to accept a temporary economic slowdown now as part of a programme for ending inflation or to experience a more severe slowdown somewhat later as a result of continued or accelerated inflation.

6 Restraint in the rate of monetary growth is both a necessary and a sufficient condition for controlling inflation. Controlling inflation, in turn, is a necessary *but not sufficient* condition for improving Britain's productivity, which is the fundamental requirement for a healthy economy. That requires measures on a broader scale to restore and improve incentives, promote productive investment, and give a greater scope for private enterprise and initiative. However, consideration of such measures is outside the scope of this enquiry.

2 Monetary Strategy

7 I strongly approve of the general outlines of the monetary strategy outlined by the Government: taking monetary growth as the major intermediate target; stating in advance targets for a number of years ahead; setting targets that require a steady and gradual reduction in monetary growth; and stressing the Government's intentions of strictly adhering to those targets.

8 The numerical targets for the growth of £M3 set forth in the *Financial Statement and Budget Report for 1980–81* (dated 26 March 1980) seem to me of the right order of magnitude, and to decline at about the right rate. This judgment rests heavily on my studies of the experience of countries other than the UK (the US, Japan, etc.), as well as on my detailed studies of the longer-run movements of British monetary and economic magnitudes (see paragraphs 21–5 below).

9 The key rôle assigned to targets for the PSBR, on the other hand, seems to me unwise for several reasons. (1) These numbers are highly misleading because of the failure to adjust for the effect of inflation.[1] (2) There is no necessary relation between the size of PSBR and monetary growth. There is currently such a relation, though even then a loose one, only because of the undesirable techniques used to control the money supply (see section C). (3) The size of the PSBR does affect the level of interest rates. However, for given monetary growth, the major effect on interest rates is exerted by the real PSBR, not the nominal PSBR. In any event, in line with the Government's announced and highly commendable policy of relying on market mechanisms, interest rates should be left to the market to determine, not be manipulated by government. (4) Emphasis on the PSBR diverts attention from the really important aspects of government fiscal policy: the fraction of the nation's output that is diverted to uses determined by government officials rather than by the individual members of the public who, for the most part, produce the output. Total government spending, not taxes and not borrowing, measures the true current cost to the citizenry of governmental activities (with only minor qualifications to allow for capital transactions). The Government has expressed the intention of reducing government spending as a fraction of national income, but the reductions projected in the *Financial Statement* seem to me too little and too late. It would be far better to cut both spending and explicit taxes more rapidly, even though that led to a higher PSBR. That might even reduce pressure on interest rates because the additional demand for credit by the Government might be more than offset by an additional supply of credit (in real terms) generated by the combination of a contemporaneous and a prospective reduction in the Government's command over resources. However, I am here departing somewhat from monetary policy proper and trespassing on policy to raise output.

3 Monetary Tactics

10 When we shift from the strategy of monetary policy to the tactics, it is essential to distinguish lip-service from a change in policy. Central bankers throughout the world have rendered lip-service to the control of monetary aggregates by announcing monetary growth targets. However, few have altered their policies to match their professions of faith. Most have continued to try to ride several horses at once by simultaneously trying to control monetary aggregates, interest rates, and foreign exchange rates – in the process introducing excessive variability into all three. And few have altered their operating procedures to make them consistent with the professed goal of controlling monetary growth. Bureaucratic inertia has been stronger than the pressure to fit actions to words. The United States is a particularly egregious example, mitigated so far only very partially by the Federal Reserve System's 6 October 1979 pronouncement.

11 The United Kingdom is another egregious example, manifested most recently in the Green Paper on *Monetary Control* (Cmnd. 7858, March 1980). I could hardly believe my eyes when I read, in the first paragraph of the summary chapter, 'The principal means of controlling the growth of the money supply must be fiscal policy – both public expenditure and tax policy – and interest rates'. Interpreted literally, this sentence is simply wrong. Only a Rip Van Winkle, who had not read any of the flood of literature during the past decade and more on the money supply process, could possibly have written that sentence. Direct control of the monetary base is an alternative to fiscal policy and interest rates as a means of controlling monetary growth. Of course, direct control of the monetary base will affect interest rates (though not in the way that is implied in Chapter 4 of the Green Paper), but that is a very different thing from controlling monetary growth through interest rates.

12 This remarkable sentence reflects the myopia engendered by long-established practices, the difficulty we all have of adjusting our outlook to changed circumstances. For most of its history, the Bank of England has regarded itself as concerned with credit conditions. Under a classical gold standard, it had no direct control over the quantity of money. That was determined by international payment flows. It could affect the quantity of money (or the monetary base) over anything but very short periods only by acting on the credit markets to alter the quantity of

money demanded. Under the fixed exchange Bretton Woods system that prevailed for most of the post-war period, the Bank's leeway was somewhat greater but still it had to operate with primary concern for the balance of payments, and hence, again, it was largely limited to operating either through foreign exchange control or on the credit markets – that is, to trying to affect the quantity of money demanded. Of course, the fact that the Bank of England had to operate under a gold standard, or chose to operate under fixed rates, did not prevent changes in the quantity of money, however produced, from having predictable effects on nominal income, output, prices, and interest rates. Indeed, as pointed out later (paragraphs 22 and 23), these reactions have been the same under various régimes for determining the quantity of money.

13 The elimination of exchange controls and the acceptance of a floating exchange rate have changed circumstances fundamentally. The balance of payments can be taken care of by the market. Of course, if the Bank sought to peg or manipulate the exchange rate, that would correspondingly limit its ability to control monetary growth. The announced policy of the Government is to refrain from such activity except 'to prevent excessive fluctuations in the exchange rate'.[2] In my opinion, this exception is a mistake; better to leave the market entirely free – certainly for such a broad and efficient market as exists in British sterling. But mistake or not, the exception, if adhered to, is minor and does not prevent the Bank from controlling the base directly.

14 The attempt to control the money supply through interest rates reflects a long-standing confusion between money and credit. Most credit is not money, by any definition of money; much money is not credit (as is clearest with a commodity standard such as gold). Bank of England notes used to be described, and perhaps still are, as 'promises to pay'. They are clearly not that today. They are simply fiat, not in any mean-ingful sense a credit instrument. Interest rates are the price of credit not the price of money. The price of money is the quantity of goods and services that will 'buy' a piece of money (the reciprocal of the price level). Manipulating interest rates may have a decided influence on the demand for credit – though even that is dubious because of the limited range of interest rates that the Bank can manipulate. But it has a highly erratic and undependable influence on the quantity of money demanded over the kind of short periods which are crucial for monetary control (periods of a few months up to a year or more). Why else has it been that central banks seeking to control monetary aggregates in this way have had so

poor a record in achieving their monetary targets, while they have had an excellent record in achieving their specific interest rate targets? Trying to control the money supply through 'fiscal policy ... and interest rates' is trying to control the output of one item (money) through altering the demand for it by manipulating the incomes of its users (that is the rôle of fiscal policy) or the prices of substitutes for it (that is the rôle of interest rates). A precise analogy is like trying to control the output of motor cars by altering the incomes of potential purchasers and manipulating rail and air fares. In principle, possible in both cases, but in practice highly inefficient. Far easier to control the output of motor cars by controlling the availability of a basic raw material, say steel, to the manufacturers – a precise analogy to controlling the money supply by controlling the availability of base money to banks and others.

15 The authorities can control the monetary base directly.[3] However, currently they have surrendered control of the base by standing ready passively to provide reserves to the banking system at the option of the banks. That is, I believe, a serious mistake. The authorities should decide directly the amount of base money, including reserves, that is issued, rather than seeking to guesstimate the terms on which a target amount will be demanded.

16 Control of the monetary base does not produce rigid and precise control of the money supply. The link between the base and the money supply is currently far too loose, thanks primarily to the institutional arrangements under which banks can hold a variety of assets to meet reserve requirements. It would be highly desirable to replace this multiple reserve system by one in which only a single asset – liabilities of the Bank of England in the form of notes or deposits (i.e. base money) – satisfies reserve requirements. This is probably the most important single change in current institutional arrangements that is required to permit more effective control of the money supply (either through controlling the base, or through the present obsolete methods). No doubt other institutional changes would help (such as some of those listed in the Green Paper on Monetary Control). That is a matter on which there are many in Britain who are far better qualified to judge than I am.

17 Control of the monetary base should be exercised through open market operations primarily in short-term debt, which, with a single reserve asset, would no longer be close to a perfect substitute for base money. There are a variety of ways in which the amounts to be purchased

or sold each week can be determined, and there is an extensive literature on alternative techniques. The key point, however, is that the Bank should decide in advance each week how much to buy or sell, not the price at which it will buy or sell. It should permit interest rates to be determined entirely by the market. (None of this would prevent temporary lender-of-last-resort operations in case of emergency.)

18 Opponents of control through the monetary base typically maintain that such a technique would lead to an undesirably wide variation in market interest rates. With respect to very short-run movements, that may be the case. But with respect to movements over periods of more than a few weeks, the result would be precisely the opposite. As in any market, the effect of pegging a price is to permit disturbances that would have been eliminated by moderate changes in price to accumulate and ultimately force major changes. Certainly, it would be hard to conceive of more erratic movements in interest rates than have occurred under the mistaken attempts by central banks to 'stabilise' rates.

19 As these remarks indicate, *debt policy* (as distinguished from the 'public expenditure and tax policy' that the Green Paper on *Monetary Control* regards as 'fiscal policy') does play a critical rôle in controlling monetary aggregates. In this respect, I have long felt that nominal gilt-edged long-term securities are a highly undesirable vehicle both for monetary policy and for funding the PSBR. Recent experience dramatically illustrates the point. The Government is committed to ending inflation. Yet it is issuing long-term securities that offer yields justified only if substantial inflation continues. Of course, the market is setting those rates and the continuance of such high rates reflects a lack of confidence in the ability of the Government to achieve its objectives. Does the Government share that lack of confidence? Are the terms on which it is offering long-dated debt a more accurate reflection of its intentions than its firm and repeated public pronouncements? If not, and if the Government succeeds in reducing inflation, it is saddling itself or its successors with unconscionably and unnecessarily high future interest payments.

20 The correct resolution of the problems raised by the preceding paragraph is either to issue *no* long-dated debt, or to issue such debt *only* in a form fully indexed for future inflation. I have long favoured such an indexed debt issue on other grounds, notably equity to lenders and smoother economic adjustment to rising inflation. The avoidance of

the problems raised in the preceding paragraph is a further powerful reason for doing so.

4 Empirical Evidence Supporting Monetary Strategy

21 The Committee indicates that it would 'particularly welcome empirical evidence whether from the UK or other countries'. Though I have nothing to offer in terms of short-term econometric models or their equivalent for the UK, studies already published by myself and collaborators provide extensive evidence on the rôle of money, and on the temporal relation between changes in monetary growth and in output and inflation. In particular, they demonstrate that the initial effect of a change in monetary growth is an offsetting movement in velocity, followed by changes in the growth of spending initially manifested in output and employment, and only later in inflation. The initial offsetting movement in velocity is misleading, since it simply reflects the lags in reaction. It is observed in velocity measured by dividing current income by the current quantity of money. It is largely or wholly absent in a velocity calculated by dividing current income by the quantity of money two or three quarters *earlier*, thereby allowing for the typical lag in reaction. The failure to allow for lags in reaction is a major source of misunderstanding. For the US, the UK, and Japan, the lag between a change in monetary growth and output is roughly six to nine months, between the change in monetary growth and inflation, roughly two years. Of course, the effects are spread out, not concentrated at the indicated point of time.

22 In an as yet unpublished study by Anna J. Schwartz and myself dealing with monetary trends in the US and the UK over the past century, we find that the demand for money, in the sense of a demand function relating the quantity of money demanded to a small number of key variables, has been highly stable over a century for both countries, once allowance is made for such episodic disturbances as major wars.[4] There are some systematic differences between the demand functions for the US and the UK, but they are minor. For most of the century, the two countries can be regarded as part of a single financial community.

23 A second, and even more striking, finding for the UK is that, for

periods as short as a cycle phase (on the average a bit less than three years), to quote from our draft manuscript,

> ... there seems little if any relation between monetary change and output: a simple quantity theory that regards price change as determined primarily by monetary change and output by independent other factors fits the evidence for the period as a whole (excluding wars ...). The whole of a change in the quantity of money is absorbed sooner or later by prices, and in the early stages more by changes in velocity than by changes in output ....[5]

Misled by the 'conventional wisdom', we expected a positive relation between price and output change and between both and monetary change, and searched long and diligently, and we believe, not simple-mindedly, to uncover such a relation. On the contrary – if the US interwar period is excluded – a negative relation between price and output change is more typical, for both statistical and economic reasons .... . We are reminded of Keynes's dictum, expressed in another connection: 'I find myself moved, not for the first time, to remind contemporary economists that the classical teaching embodied some permanent truths of great significance, which we are liable today to overlook because we associate them with other doctrines which we cannot now accept without much qualification. There are in these matters deep undercurrents at work, natural forces, or even the invisible hand, which are operating towards equilibrium' [*Economic Journal*, June 1946, p. 185].

We have concluded that the widely held belief in a positive relation between price and output change and in the inadequacy of the quantity theory stem largely from a tendency to regard the US interwar period as the norm rather than, as we found it, idiosyncratic. That period generated Keynes's *General Theory* and sparked the Keynesian Revolution. It appears that Keynes's theory, far from being general, is highly special, a view that has often been expressed but seldom documented as fully as we believe we have been able to.

24   Another finding from the monetary trends study that is relevant to exchange rates is with respect to the relation between the market exchange rate and the purchasing-power exchange rate. Government intervention in the exchange market since the 1930s has been more potent in increasing discrepancies between the two rates than improvements in transportation and communication have been in reducing them. I have discussed this finding in my Harry G. Johnson Memorial Lecture.[6] Fortunately, the Government's abolition of exchange control and freeing of the exchange rate promises to end this unfortunate situation, which has been so potent a source of instability.

5 Brief Comments on Questions Not Covered Above

25 This section contains brief answers to many of the specific questions in the Committee's questionnaire that have not been covered sufficiently in the earlier sections of this memorandum. I apologise for the brevity and dogmatic form of the answers, but time limitations render full answers, embodying all academic qualifications, impossible. I designate the questions by the letters and numbers used in the questionnaire.

A. Q1:   Of course, the Government should 'still pursue these' and many other objectives. The key question is different. What are the best means of achieving its objectives? It does not follow that attacking them directly is a desirable means. It is my opinion, as it is of the Government, that the most effective means open to the Government consists of providing a framework that will encourage and support a healthy and vigorous free private market. That requires ending inflation, eliminating governmental obstacles to the effective operation of the market, reducing the government's essential functions of protecting the country against coercion by other countries, protecting individuals against coercion by their fellow citizens, enforcing private contracts and mediating disputes, and, in the words of Adam Smith, 'erecting and maintaining certain public works and certain public institutions, which it can never be for the interest of any individual, or small number of individuals, to erect and maintain'.

A. Q3:   The post-war commitment to high employment has led to high unemployment! The way to foster productive employment at a high level is to end the counter-productive policies that the government has followed, largely in the name of 'full employment'.

B. Q2:   There is, in my opinion, no case whatsoever for direct controls on credit.

B. Q4:   Controlling the money supply is *not* a mechanism for controlling the economy. It is a means of providing a stable monetary framework for an economy, including the control of inflation.

B. Q9: This is a highly complex question, to which the following answer is an oversimplified response: the desirable trend path of the PSBR should be to achieve and then maintain a zero ratio of the real PSBR to GNP. The PSBR should be allowed to vary automatically over the cycle in response to cyclical variations in the nominal volume of government spending for a stable expenditure programme and of government receipts for a stable tax structure. Neither expenditure programmes nor tax structures should be varied in response to cyclical fluctuations. The PSBR should not be modified in response to changes in the personal saving ratio.

B. Q11 and Q12: I strongly disagree. Monetary policy actions affect asset portfolios in the first instance, spending decisions in the second, which translate into effects on output and then on prices. The changes in exchange rates are in turn mostly a response to these effects of home policy and of similar policy abroad. This question is topsy-turvy. Floating exchange rates are necessary in order for a monetary policy proper to be possible. They are a facilitating mechanism not a 'transmission mechanism'. Fixed rates render an independent monetary policy impossible, as Keynes pointed out in his 1923 *Monetary Reform*.

B. Q13: No.

B. Q14: No, hampered rather than assisted.

B. Q17: Unemployment and excess capacity are an unfortunate side-effect of reducing inflation not a cure – just as staying in bed is a side-effect of an appendicitis operation, not a cure for appendicitis. Insofar as unemployment and excess capacity have a direct effect on inflation it is to make inflation worse by reducing output growth. The mechanism causing the contraction in output is the slowing of nominal spending in response to the slowing of monetary growth and the inevitable lags in the absorption of slower spending by wages and prices. These lags arise partly from the existence of long-term contracts and of legal obstacles to changes in prices and wages, partly from the persistence of inflationary expectations, and partly from other sources.

B. Q18:   The best evidence is from the prior experience of the UK and other countries. As I read that experience, of which that described in paragraph 24 and the experience of Japan since 1973 seem to me most relevant, I conclude that (a) only a modest reduction in output and employment will be a side-effect of reducing inflation to single figures by 1982, and (b) the effect on investment and the potential for future growth will be highly favourable.

C. Q2:   The policy of relying on market mechanisms proclaimed by the Government is precisely such a flexible policy. The feedback is automatic and its strength is proportioned to the reaction required. It does not require being 'easily understood' by either the private sector or governmental civil servants to be effective. Yet I suspect it is far more 'easily understood' by the private sector than the alternative policies that the Government has been following with such a notable lack of success.

C. Q3:   No.

C. Q4:   Yes, I regard steady monetary growth and the maintenance of a favourable framework for free and flexible private markets as the most 'robust' policies available.

Notes

1   See C. T. Taylor and A. R. Threadgold, '"Real" national saving and its sectoral composition', Bank of England Discussion Paper No. 6, October 1979.
2   Letter from the Chancellor of the Exchequer on Monetary Policy, Treasury and Civil Service Committee, *Memoranda on Monetary Policy and Public Expenditure*, 19 February 1980, p.3.
3   See for example, Brian Griffiths, 'The Reform of Monetary Control in the United Kingdom', City University Centre for Banking and International Finance, *Annual Monetary Review*, No. 1 (October 1979), pp. 28–41: and

W. Greenwell Associates, *Special Monetary Bulletin, Monetary Base Control*, 21 April 1980, p.3.

4   Our study, under the auspices of the National Bureau of Economic Research, covers experience over the past century on the relation between monetary and other economic magnitudes, such as nominal income, prices, output, and interest rates, with special emphasis on a comparison of the US and the UK. Many of our findings are highly relevant to intermediate and long-term policy, less so to very short-term policy since in order to eliminate short-term cyclical perturbations, we take the cycle phase (a cyclical expansion or a cyclical contraction) as our basic unit of analysis. All our data have been converted into averages for such phases.

5   Let me emphasise that this conclusion is not inconsistent with my earlier assertion (paragraph 5) that 'a successful policy of reducing inflation will have as an unavoidable side-effect a temporary retardation in economic growth'. The reconciliation is that the 'temporary' retardation lasts less than a cycle phase and is averaged out in our data.

6   'Prices of Money and Goodss across Frontiers: the £ and $ over a Century', *The World Economy* 2 (4), February 1980, pp.497–511.

4

Unemployment versus Inflation? – an Evaluation of the Phillips Curve

The discussion of the Phillips curve started with truth in 1926, proceeded through error some 30 years later, and by now has returned back to 1926 and to the original truth. That is about 50 years for a complete circuit. You can see how technological development has speeded up the process of both producing and dissipating ignorance.

1 Fisher and Phillips

I choose the year 1926 not at random but because in that year Irving Fisher published an article in the *International Labour Review* under the title 'A Statistical Relation between Unemployment and Price Changes'.[1]

The Fisher approach

Fisher's article dealt with precisely the same empirical phenomenon that Professor A. W. Phillips analysed in his celebrated article in *Economica* some 32 years later.[2] Both were impressed with the empirical observation that inflation tended to be associated with low levels of unemployment and deflation with high levels. One amusing item in Fisher's article from a very different point of view is that he starts out by saying that he has been so deeply interested in this subject that 'during the last three years in particular I have had at least one computer in my office almost

Published originally as IEA Occasional Paper No.44 (1975)

constantly at work on this project'.[3] Of course what he meant was a human being operating a calculating machine.

There was, however, a crucial difference between Fisher's analysis and Phillips's, between the truth of 1926 and the error of 1958, which had to do with the direction of causation. Fisher took *the rate of change of prices* to be the independent variable that set the process going. In his words,

> When the dollar is losing value, or in other words when the price level is rising, a business man finds his receipts rising as fast, on the average, as this general rise of prices, but not his expenses, because his expenses consist, to a large extent, of things which are contractually fixed ...Employment is then stimulated – for a time at least.[4]

To elaborate his analysis and express it in more modern terms, let anything occur that produces a higher level of spending – or, more precisely, a higher rate of increase in spending than was anticipated. Producers would at first interpret the faster rate of increase in spending as an increase in real demand for their product. The producers of shoes, hats, or coats would discover that apparently there was an increase in the amount of goods they could sell at pre-existing prices. No one of them would know at first whether the change was affecting him in particular or whether it was general. In the first instance, each producer would be tempted to expand output, as Fisher states, and also to allow prices to rise. But at first much or most of the unanticipated increase in nominal demand (i.e. demand expressed in £s) would be absorbed by increases (or faster increases) in employment and output rather than by increases (or faster increases) in prices. Conversely, for whatever reason, let the rate of spending slow down, or rise less rapidly than was anticipated, and each individual producer would in the first instance interpret the slowdown at least partly as reflecting something peculiar to him. The result would be partly a slowdown in output and a rise in unemployment and partly a slowdown in prices.

Fisher was describing a *dynamic* process arising out of fluctuations in the rate of spending about some average trend or norm. He went out of his way to emphasise the importance of distinguishing between 'high and low prices on the one hand and the rise and fall of prices on the other'.[5] He put it that way because he was writing at a time when a stable level of prices was taken to be the norm. Were he writing today, he would emphasise the distinction between the rate of inflation and changes in the rate of inflation. (And perhaps some future writer will have to emphasise the difference between the second and the third derivatives!) The important distinction – and it is quite clear that this is what Fisher had in mind – is between *anticipated* and *unanticipated* changes.

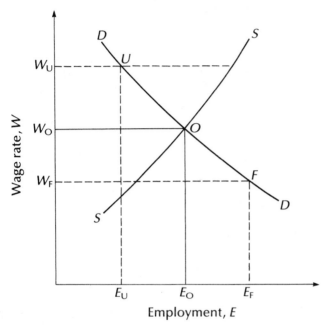

Figure 1.

The Phillips approach

Professor Phillips's approach was from exactly the opposite direction. He took the level of *employment* to be the independent variable that set the process going. He treated the rate of change of wages as the dependent variable. His argument was a very simple analysis – I hesitate to say simple-minded, but so it has proved – in terms of *static* supply and demand conditions. He said:

> When the demand for a commodity or service is high relatively to the supply of it we expect the price to rise, the rate of rise being greater the greater the excess demand ... It seems plausible that this principle should

operate as one of the factors determining the rate of change of money wage rates, which are the price of labour services.[6]

Phillips's approach is based on the usual (*static*) demand and supply curves as illustrated in figure 1. At the point of intersection, O, the market is in equilibrium at the wage-rate W_O, with the amount of labour employed E_O equal to the amount of labour demanded. Unemployment is zero – which is to say, as measured, equal to 'frictional' or 'transitional' unemployment, or to use the terminology I adopted some years ago from Wicksell, at its 'natural' rate. At this point, says Phillips, there is no upward pressure on wages. Consider instead the point F, where the quantity of labour demanded is higher than the quantity supplied. There is over-employment, wages at W_F are below the equilibrium level, and there will be upward pressure on them. At point U, there is unemployment, W_U is above the equilibrium wage-rate and there is downward pressure. The larger the discrepancy between the quantity of labour demanded and the quantity supplied, the stronger the pressure and hence the more rapidly wages will rise or fall.

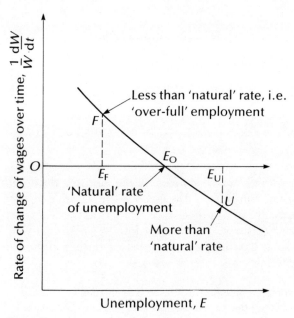

Figure 2.

Phillips translated this analysis into an observable relation by plotting the level of unemployment on one axis, and the rate of change of wages over time on the other, as in figure 2. Point E_O corresponds to point O in figure 1. Unemployment is at its 'natural' rate so wages are stable (or in a growing economy, rising at a rate equal to the rate of productivity growth). Point F corresponds to 'over-full' employment, so wages are rising; point U to unemployment, so wages are falling.

Fisher talked about price changes, Phillips about wage changes, but I believe that for our purpose that is not an important distinction. Both Fisher and Phillips took it for granted that wages are a major component of total cost and that prices and wages would tend to move together. So both of them tended to go very readily from rates of wage change to rate of price change and I shall do so as well.

The fallacy in Phillips

Phillips's analysis seems very persuasive and obvious, yet is utterly fallacious. It is fallacious because no economic theorist has ever asserted that the demand and supply of labour were functions of the *nominal* wage rate (i.e. wage rate expressed in £s). Every economic theorist from Adam Smith to the present would have told you that the vertical axis in figure 1 should refer not to the *nominal* wage rate but to the *real* wage rate.

But once you label the vertical axis $\dfrac{W}{P}$ as in figure 3, the graph has nothing to say about what is going to happen to *nominal wages* or prices. There is not even any *prima facie* presumption that it has anything to say. For example, consider point O in figure 3. At that level of employment, there is neither upward nor downward pressure on the real wage. But that real wage can remain constant with W and P separately *constant*, or with W and P each *rising* at the rate of 10 per cent a year, or *falling* at the rate of 10 per cent a year, or doing anything else, provided both change at the *same* rate.

2 The Keynesian Confusion Between Nominal and Real Wages

How did a sophisticated mind like Phillips's – and he was certainly a highly sophisticated and subtle economist – come to confuse nominal wages with real wages? He was led to do so by the general intellectual

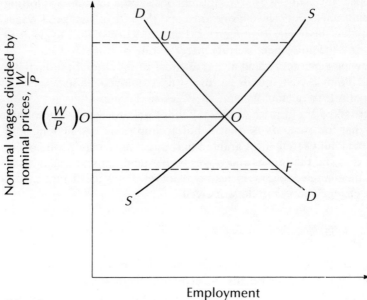

Figure 3.

climate that had been engendered by the Keynesian revolution. From this point of view, the essential element of the Keynesian revolution was the assumption that prices are highly rigid relative to output so that a change in demand of the kind considered by Fisher would be reflected almost entirely in *output* and very little in prices. The price level could be regarded as an institutional datum. The simple way to interpret Phillips is that he was therefore assuming the change in nominal wages to be equal to the change in real wages.

But that is not really what he was saying. What he was saying was slightly more sophisticated. It was that changes in *anticipated* nominal wages were equal to changes in *anticipated* real wages. There were two components of the Keynesian system that were essential to his construction: first, the notion that prices are rigid in the sense that people in planning their behaviour do not allow for the possibility that the price level might change, and hence regard a change in nominal wages or nominal prices as a change in real wages and real prices; second, that real wages *ex post* could be altered by *unanticipated* inflation. Indeed, the whole Keynesian argument for the possibility of a full employment policy arose out of the supposition that it was possible to get workers (at least in the 1930s when Keynes wrote *The General Theory*) to accept lower real wages produced by inflation that they would not have accepted in the direct form of a reduction in nominal wages.[7]

These two components imply a sharp distinction between *anticipated* nominal and real wages and *actual* nominal and real wages. In the Keynesian climate of the time, it was natural for Phillips to take this distinction for granted, and to regard anticipated nominal and real wages as moving together.

I do not criticise Phillips for doing this. Science is possible only because at any one time there is a body of conventions or views or ideas that are taken for granted and on which scientists build. If each individual writer were to go back and question all the premises that underlie what he is doing, nobody would ever get anywhere. I believe that some of the people who have followed in his footsteps deserve much more criticism than he does for not noting the importance of this theoretical point once it was pointed out to them.

At any rate, it was this general intellectual climate that led Phillips to think in terms of nominal rather than real wages. The intellectual climate was also important in another direction. The Keynesian system, as everybody knows, is incomplete. It lacks an equation. A major reason for the prompt and rapid acceptance of the Phillips curve approach was the widespread belief that it provided the missing equation that connected the real system with the monetary system. In my opinion, this belief is false. What is needed to complete the Keynesian system is an equation that determines the equilibrium price level. But the Phillips curve deals with the relation between a rate of change of prices or wages and the level of unemployment. It does not determine an equilibrium price level. At any rate, the Phillips curve was widely accepted and was seized on immediately for policy purposes.[8] It is still widely used for this purpose as supposedly describing a 'trade-off', from a policy point of view, between inflation and unemployment.

It was said that what the Phillips curve means is that we are faced with a choice. If we choose a low level of inflation, say, stable prices, we shall have to reconcile ourselves to a high level of unemployment. If we choose a low level of unemployment, we shall have to reconcile ourselves to a high rate of inflation.

3 Reaction against the Keynesian System

Three developments came along in this historical account to change attitudes and to raise some questions.

One was the general theoretical reaction against the Keynesian system which brought out into the open the fallacy in the original Phillips curve approach of identifying nominal and real wages.

The second development was the failure of the Phillips curve relation to hold for other bodies of data. Fisher had found it to hold for the United States for the period before 1925; Phillips had found it to hold for Britain for a long period. But, lo and behold, when people tried it for any other place they never obtained good results. Nobody was able to construct a decent empirical Phillips curve for other circumstances. I may be exaggerating a bit – no doubt there are other successful cases; but certainly a large number of attempts were unsuccessful.

The third and most recent development is the emergence of 'stag-flation', which rendered somewhat ludicrous the confident statements that many economists had made about 'trade-offs', based on empirically fitted Phillips curves.

Short- and long-run Phillips curves

The empirical failures and the theoretical reaction produced an attempt to rescue the Phillips curve approach by distinguishing a short-run from a long-run Phillips curve. Because both potential employers and potential employees envisage an implicit or explicit employment contract covering a fairly long period, both must guess in advance what real wage will correspond to a given nominal wage. Both therefore must form anticipations about the future price level. The real wage rate that is plotted on the vertical axis of the demand and supply curve diagram is thus not the *current* real wage but the *anticipated* real wage. If we suppose that anticipations about the price level are slow to change, while the nominal wage can change rapidly and is known with little time-lag, we can, for *short* periods, revert essentially to Phillips's original formulation, except that the equilibrium position is no longer a constant nominal wage, but a nominal wage changing at the same rate as the anticipated rate of change in prices (plus, for a growing economy, the anticipated rate of change in productivity). Changes in demand and supply will then show up first in a changed rate of change of nominal wages, which will mean also in anticipated real wages. Current prices may adjust as rapidly as or more rapidly than wages, so real wages *actually* received may move in the opposite direction from nominal wages, but *anticipated* real wages will move in the same direction.

One way to put this in terms of the Phillips curve is to plot on the vertical axis not the change in nominal wages but that change minus the anticipated rate of change in prices, as in the revised figure 2, where

$$\left(\frac{1}{P} \frac{dP}{dt} \right)^*,$$

standing for the anticipated rate of change in prices, is subtracted from $(1/W)\,(dW/dt)$. This curve now tells a story much more like Fisher's original story than Phillips's. Suppose, to start with, the economy is at

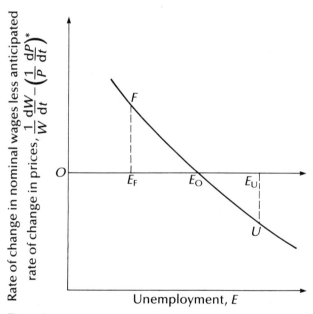

Figure 4

point E_O, with both prices and wages stable (abstracting from growth). Suppose something, say, a monetary expansion, starts nominal aggregate demand growing, which in turn produces a rise in prices and wages at the rate of, say, 2 per cent per year. Workers will initially interpret this as a rise in their real wage – because they still anticipate constant prices – and so will be willing to offer more labour (move up their supply curve), i.e. employment grows and unemployment falls. Employers may have the same anticipations as workers about the general price level, but they are more directly concerned about the price of the products they are producing and far better informed about that. They will initially interpret a rise in the demand for and price of their product as a rise in its relative price and as implying a fall in the real wage rate they must pay measured in terms of their product. They will therefore be willing to hire more labour (move down their demand curve). The combined result is a movement, say, to point F, which corresponds with 'over-full' employ-

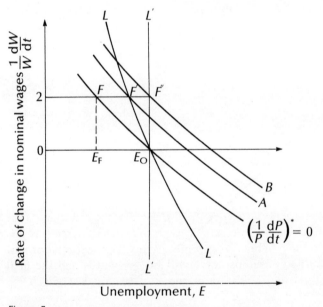

Figure 5.

ment, with nominal wages rising at 2 per cent per year.

But, as time passes, both employers and employees come to recognise that prices *in general* are rising. As Abraham Lincoln said, you can fool all of the people some of the time, you can fool some of the people all of the time, but you can't fool all of the people all of the time. As a result, they raise their estimate of the anticipated rate of inflation, which reduces the rate of rise of anticipated real wages, and leads you to slide down the curve back ultimately to the point E_O. There is thus a *short-run* 'trade-off' between inflation and unemployment, but *no long-run* 'trade-off'.

By incorporating price anticipations into the Phillips curve as I have just done, I have implicitly begged one of the main issues in the recent controversy about the Phillips curve. Thanks to recent experience of 'stagflation' plus theoretical analysis, everyone now admits that the apparent short-run Phillips curve is misleading and seriously overstates the *short*-run trade-off, but many are not willing to accept the view that the *long*-run trade-off is *zero*.

We can examine this issue by using a different way of incorporating price anticipations into the Phillips curve. Figure 4 keeps the rate of change of nominal wages on the vertical axis but contains a series of different curves, one for each anticipated rate of growth of wages. To put it algebraically, instead of writing the Phillips curve relation as

$$\frac{1}{W}\frac{dW}{dt} = \left(\frac{1}{P}\frac{dP}{dt}\right)^* = f(U), \qquad (1)$$

where U is unemployment, we can write it in more general form as

$$\frac{1}{W}\frac{dW}{dt} = f\left[U, \left(\frac{1}{P}\frac{dP}{dt}\right)^*\right]. \qquad (2)$$

Now suppose something occurs to put the economy at point F at which wages are rising at 2 per cent a year and unemployment is less than the natural rate. Then, as people adjust their expectations of inflation, the short-run Phillips curve will shift upwards and the final resting place would be on that short-run Phillips curve at which the anticipated rate of inflation equals the current rate. The issue now becomes whether that Phillips curve is like A, so that the long-run curve is negatively sloping, like LL, in which case an anticipated rate of inflation of 2 per cent will still reduce the level of unemployment, though not by as much as an unanticipated rate of 2 per cent, or whether it is like B, so that the long-run curve is *vertical*, that is, unemployment is the *same* at a 2 per cent anticipated rate of inflation as at a zero per cent anticipated rate.

4 No Long-run Money Illusion

In my Presidential Address to the American Economic Association seven years ago, I argued that the long-run Phillips curve was vertical, largely on the grounds I have already sketched here: in effect, the absence of any long-run money illusion.[9] At about the same time, Professor E. S. Phelps, now of Columbia University, offered the same hypothesis, on different though related grounds.[10] This hypothesis has come to be called the 'accelerationist' hypothesis or the 'natural rate' hypothesis. It has been called accelerationist because a policy of trying to hold unemployment below the horizontal intercept of the long-run vertical Phillips curve must lead to an *accelerated* inflation.

Suppose, beginning at point E_O on figure 4, when nobody anticipated any inflation, it is decided to aim at a lower unemployment level, say E_F. This can be done initially by producing an inflation of 2 per cent, as shown by moving along the Phillips curve corresponding to anticipations of no inflation. But, as we have seen, the economy will not stay at F because people's anticipations will shift, and if the rate of inflation were kept at 2 per cent, the economy would be driven back to the level of unemployment it started with. The only way unemployment can be kept below the 'natural rate' is by an *ever-accelerating* inflation, which always keeps current inflation ahead of anticipated inflation. Any resemblance between that analysis and what you in Britain have been observing in practice is not coincidental: what recent British governments have tried to do is to keep unemployment below the natural rate, and to do so they have had to accelerate inflation – from 3.9 per cent in 1964 to 16.0 per cent in 1974, according to your official statistics.[11]

Misunderstandings about the 'natural rate' of unemployment

The hypothesis came to be termed the 'natural rate' hypothesis because of the emphasis on the natural rate of unemployment. The term 'the natural rate' has been misunderstood. It does not refer to some *irreducible minimum* of unemployment. It refers rather to that rate of employment which is consistent with the *existing real conditions* in the labour market. It can be lowered by removing obstacles in the labour market, by reducing friction. It can be raised by introducing additional obstacles. The purpose of the concept is to separate the monetary from the non-monetary aspects of the employment situation – precisely the same purpose that Wicksell had in using the word 'natural' in connection with the rate of interest.

In the past few years, a large number of statistical studies have investigated the question whether the long-run Phillips curve is or is not vertical. That dispute is still in train.

Most of the statistical tests were undertaken by rewriting equation (2) in the form:

$$\frac{1}{W}\frac{dW}{dt} = a + b\left(\frac{1}{P}\frac{dP}{dt}\right)^* + f(U)$$

or

$$\frac{1}{P}\frac{dP}{dt} = a + b\left(\frac{1}{P}\frac{dP}{dt}\right)^* + f(U),\tag{3}$$

where the left-hand side was either the rate of change of wages or the rate of change of prices. The question then asked was the value of b.[12] The original Phillips curve essentially assumed $b = 0$; the acceleration hypothesis set b equal to 1. The authors of the various tests I am referring to used observed data, mostly time-series data, to estimate the numerical value of b.[13] Almost every such test has come out with a numerical value of b less than 1, implying that there is a long-run 'trade-off'.[14] However, there are a number of difficulties with these tests, some on a rather superficial level, others on a much more fundamental level.

One obvious statistical problem is that the statistically fitted curves have not been the same for different periods of fit and have produced very unreliable extrapolations for periods subsequent to the period of fit. So it looks very much as if the statistical results are really measuring a *short*-term relationship despite the objective. The key problem here is that, in order to make the statistical test, it is necessary to have some measure of the anticipated rate of inflation. Hence, every such test is a joint test of the accelerationist hypothesis and a particular hypothesis about the formation of anticipations.

5 The Adaptive Expectations Hypothesis

Most of these statistical tests embody the so-called adaptive expectations hypothesis, which has worked well in many problems. It states that anticipations are revised on the basis of the difference between the current rate of inflation and the anticipated rate. If the anticipated rate was, say, 5 per cent but the current rate 10 per cent, the anticipated rate will be revised upward by some fraction of the difference between 10 and 5. As is well known, this implies that the anticipated rate of inflation is an exponentially weighted average of past rates of inflation, the weights declining as one goes back in time.

Even on their own terms, then, these results are capable of two different interpretations. One is that the long-run Phillips curve is not vertical but has a negative slope. The other is that this has not been a satisfactory method of evaluating people's expectations for this purpose.

A somewhat more subtle statistical problem with these equations is that, if the accelerationist hypothesis is correct, the results are either estimates of a short-run curve or are statistically unstable. Suppose the true value of b is unity. Then when current inflation equals anticipated inflation, which is the definition of a long-run curve, we have that

$$f(U) = -a. \tag{4}$$

This is the vertical long-run Phillips curve with the value of U that satisfies it being the natural rate of unemployment. Any other values of U reflect either short-term equilibrium positions or a stochastic component in the natural rate. But the estimation process used, with $(1/P)$ (dP/dt) on the left-hand side, treats different observed rates of unemployment as if they were exogenous, as if they could persist indefinitely. There is simply no way of deriving equation (4) from such an approach. In effect, the implicit assumption that unemployment can take different values begs the whole question raised by the accelerationist hypothesis. On a statistical level, this approach requires putting U, or a function of U, on the left-hand side, not $(1/P)$ (dP/dt).

6 Rational Expectations

A still more fundamental criticism has recently been made by a number of economists in the United States. This criticism has its origin in an important article by John Muth on rational expectations. The rational expectations approach has been applied to the problem in recent articles by Robert Lucas of Carnegie – Mellon (now of Chicago), Tom Sargent of the University of Minnesota, and a number of others.[15]

This criticism is that you cannot take seriously the notion that people form anticipations on the basis of a weighted average of past experience

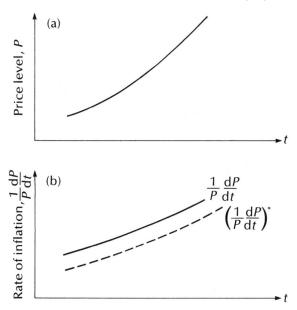

Figure 5.

with fixed weights – or any other scheme that is inconsistent with the way inflation is really being generated. For example, let us suppose that the current course of the price level is the one drawn in figure 5(a), that inflation is accelerating. With a fixed exponential weighting pattern (with weights summing to unity) the anticipated rate of inflation will always be lagging behind, as in figure 5(b). But people who are forming anticipations are not fools – or at least some of them are not. They are not going to *persist* in being wrong. And more generally they are not going to base their anticipations solely on the past history of prices. Is there anybody in this room whose anticipation of inflation next year will be independent of the result of the coming British elections? That is not reported in the past record of prices. Will it be independent of policies announced by the parties that come into power, and so on? Therefore, said Muth, we should assume that people form their anticipations on the basis of a correct economic theory: not that they are right in *each individual* case but that over any long period they will *on the average* be right. Sometimes this will lead to the formation of anticipations on the basis of adaptive expectations, but by no means always.

If you apply that idea to the present problem it turns out that, if the true world is one in which people form expectations on a rational basis so that on the average they are right, then assuming that they form expectations by averaging the past with fixed weights will yield a value of b in equation (3) less than unity even though the true value is unity.

Consider a world in which there is a vertical long-run Phillips curve and in which people form their expectations rationally, so that on the average, over a long period, their expectations are equal to what happens. In such a world, the statistician comes along and estimates equation (3) on the assumption that people form their anticipations by averaging past experience with fixed weights. What will he find? It turns out that he will find that b is less than 1. Of course, this possibility does not prove that the statistical tests incorporating adaptive expectations are wrong but only provides an alternative interpretation of their results.

In a series of very interesting and important papers, Lucas and Sargent[16] have explored the implication of the rational expectations hypothesis and have tried to derive empirical tests of the slope of the long-run Phillips curve without the possibly misleading assumption of adaptive expectations.

Their empirical tests use a different kind of information. For example, one implication of a rational expectations hypothesis is that, in a country in which prices have fluctuated a great deal, expectations will respond to changes in the current rate of inflation much more rapidly than in a country in which prices have been relatively stable. It follows that the observed short-run Phillips curve will be steeper in the first country than in the second. Comparisons among countries in this way, as well as other tests, seem so far entirely consistent with what any reasonable man must surely expect: which is that, *since you can't fool all the people all the time, the true long-run Phillips curve is vertical.*

7 Implications for Theory and Policy

The evidence is by no means all in. Some of the articles I have referred to are not yet published and some have been published only in the past two or three years. So we certainly cannot regard the matter as settled. Even so, it is worth noting how far-reaching are the implications of this view not only for the Phillips curve problem but also for policy.

One very strong and very important implication for policy is that, if you treat people as forming expectations on a rational basis, no fixed rule of monetary or fiscal policy will enable you to achieve anything other than the natural rate of unemployment. And you can see why. Because – to go back to my initial Phillips curve analysis – the only way in which you ever get a reduction of unemployment is through *unanticipated* inflation.

If the government follows any fixed rule whatsoever, *so long as the people know it*, they will be able to take it into account. And consequently you cannot achieve an unemployment target other than the natural rate by any fixed rule. The only way you can do so is by continually being cleverer than all the people, by continually making up *new* rules and using them for a while until people catch up on them. Then you must invent a new set of rules. That is not a very promising possibility.

This analysis provides a different sort of intellectual background for a view that some of us have held for a long time: that it is a better approach to policy to say that you are going to co-operate with the people and inform them of what you are doing, so giving them a basis for their judgements, rather than trying to fool them. What the Sargent/Lucas argument and analysis really suggests is that you are fooling yourself if you think that you can fool them.

That is about where the present state of the argument is. I might summarise by saying that there is essentially no economist any longer who believes in the naïve Phillips curve of the kind originally proposed. The argument has shifted now to a second level, where everybody agrees that the long-run Phillips curve is steeper than the short-run Phillips curve. The only argument is whether it is vertical or not quite so vertical. And here the evidence is not quite all in. But there is a line of approach in analysis and reasoning which enables you to interpret, so far as I know, all the existing evidence consistently on the hypothesis of a long-run vertical Phillips curve.

8 Addendum: Questions and Answers on the Trade Unions and Inflation

LORD (WILFRED) BROWN: Can one leave trade union power out of account in all these equations?

PROFESSOR FRIEDMAN: I will quote from another famous American writer, a humorist and not an economist, who said, 'The trouble with people ain't ignorance, it's what they know that ain't so.' Trade unions play a very important rôle in determining the position of the natural level of unemployment. They play a more important rôle in denying opportunities to some classes in the community that are open to others. They play a very important rôle in the structure of the labour force and the structure of *relative* wages. But, despite appearances to the contrary, a *given* amount of trade union power does not play any rôle in exacerbating inflation. It is true that if relatively weak unions become strong, *in the process of going from weak to strong* they may exert an interim inflationary influence. They will, in the process, drive up the real wages of their members. This will reduce the level of employment in their sector. Insofar as the government has a full employment policy and is sensitive to the total level of unemployment, it will adopt expansionary policies and drive up the level of money demand. This is capable of producing a *temporary* rise to a new level of prices. But it does not produce continuing inflation. The strong union will then get its new real wage rate, and there will be a re-alignment of employment in the various industries.

What seems so obvious ought to be judged against a broader range of experience. If A produces B, then where you have A you should have B. If A is the only factor that produces B, then where you have B you should have A. If you look around the world and at your own (British) experience, and our (American) experience, you will find there are many periods when you had strong unions and there was no inflation. There are many periods when you had no unions and a great deal of inflation. Historically there simply is nothing like a one-to-one relationship between strong trade unions and inflation.

Let me explain the fallacy in the argument as I see it. I think you will agree that strong industrial monopolies do not produce inflation; they produce high relative prices for the products they are monopolising, and low output for those products. If a monopoly gets stronger, or if a monopoly replaces competition, in the process of going from competition to monopoly, it will drive up the relative price of its product and reduce the output. If there is difficulty in absorbing the redundant employees created in that way, once again there may be a once-for-all rise in the price level, but there is no *continuous* process of inflation.

Why are unions different? People say, because unions are not max-imising profit. But that is not really relevant. Union behaviour is not an utterly random, erratic thing; it is determined by some objectives, whatever they may be. The question you must ask is: Is there an equilibrium real wage? Analysis of that problem shows the fallacy in the more sophisticated arguments that propose to demonstrate unions' responsibility for inflation.

Suppose that all union agreements run for three years, and that, whenever they are negotiated, they include a provision for a 100 per cent cost-of-living adjustment. Then unions are truly negotiating for real wages. How can strong unions under those circumstances create inflation? There is no way. A strong union can create social conflict, it can drive people out of work, it can create unemployment. If it becomes stronger, and therefore the number of people employed in its areas is going to be smaller as it is driving up its real wage, it can create temporary inflation in the process because of some policy which is absorbing the unemployed without a wage decrease. But it cannot create *continuing* inflation.

I may say I am absolutely appalled by the widespread belief I find in Britain that you can use the paper club of price and wage control to beat down the rigid power of trade unions, that you can do by subterfuge and in indirect ways what you are not prepared to do directly and openly.

MARK BRADY: What is the possibility that a process of inflation, by producing a misallocation of resources and malinvestment, will raise the natural rate of unemployment so that the Phillips curve will be bent to the *right* rather than be vertical?

PROFESSOR FRIEDMAN: That is a very difficult question to answer. The crucial problem arises whether the inflation is open or repressed. If the inflation is open – if there are no restrictions – there is no reason why it should produce malinvestment. It will produce a maldistribution of resources by inducing people to hold smaller cash balances than they otherwise would, by inducing them to waste resources in doing physically what could be done with the aid of money. That would make the level of *real income* lower than it otherwise would be, but there is no reason why it should alter the level of employment or unemployment. That is a different question.

In order to determine the effect on *employment* you would have to know whether the activities that are substituted for money operate in a labour market with different frictional characteristics from those in other industries.

Similarly, it is not clear what will happen to the rate of growth. The level of output will always be lower with high inflation than with low inflation, but that does not mean that output may not be growing at the same rate.

In practice, inflation is not likely to be open. In my opinion far more harm is done by the measures which are taken to repress inflation than is done by the open inflation itself. Consequently, if you are realistically going to consider different rates of inflation, then I believe that what you are saying is correct, not because of the inflation, but because the higher the rate of inflation the more widespread is likely to be the government interference in the market. In effect, such interference is equivalent to increasing the amount of frictions and obstacles in the labour market, and therefore does tend to create a higher level of unemployment. That is why, when reporters and others ask how much unemployment it will cost to reduce inflation, I say to them, when did you last beat your wife? How much unemployment will it cost *not* to beat inflation?

You must not let yourself be carried away by the naïve Phillips curve approach and suppose that there really is a trade-off here. Given the way in which the political and economic structure will adapt itself to different rates of inflation, *if you continue to let inflation accelerate you are going to have higher unemployment either way.* So you only have a choice between which way you want the unemployment to come. Do you want it to come while you are getting sicker or do you want it to come while you are getting better?

QUESTION (speaker's identity unknown):   How do you reconcile the following situation with what you have just said? Supposing you have a situation with a firm or industry employing, say, 20,000 people, and unions are pressing up the wages. And then government controls the price at which the product is being sold. There comes a point where the firm says to the government: 'We cannot produce this any more, give us a subsidy.' Is not that inflation because of falling production and/or more money being pushed around?

PROFESSOR FRIEDMAN: The subsidy itself is not inflation. If the subsidy is financed by printing money the consequence will be inflation. If the subsidy is financed by taxing somebody else to pay the subsidy there is no inflation.

I am not saying that the existence of strong unions may not be one of the factors that, by a variety of devices, affects what monetary policy is. But in this respect it is just one of many influences. What produces the inflation is not trade unions, nor monopolistic employers, but what happens to the quantity of money. Anything else *that affects the quantity of money* will have the same effect.

Moreover, I go further. I can speak more confidently of my own country than I can of yours. In my country the theoretical possibilities we have discussed here – that union-caused unemployment would produce reactions on the part of governments which would promote inflation – have *not* empirically been the source of inflation. In the US the experience is that union wages have tended to lag *behind* inflation rather than to precede it. Almost all union confrontations have been 'catch-ups'. Unions have been blamed for inflation for the same reason that in this country your government blames the price of oil for inflation. Every government looks for scapegoats for its own deficiencies. That is what has happened in my country. It is what has happened in Britain.

I doubt that, in practice, any large part of your inflationary problem has been produced by mischievous unions. No doubt there have been many mischievous actions; I am not saying there have not. I am not trying to defend unions, far from it. I think they do an enormous amount of harm. But I believe that we do no good by using bad reasons for good objectives. We ought to face up to the problem of the correct policy about unions, on the relevant grounds that unions deny people opportunities to employ their resources in the most effective way and keep the standard of life of the ordinary people of Britain lower than it otherwise would be, but not on the utterly false and irrelevant grounds that in some way they are manufacturers of money and of inflation.

We must not suppose we are dealing with a completely new phenomenon. Inflations have been with us for two thousand years. The inflation in Diocletian's time was not produced by strong trade unions! Nor were almost any of the other historical inflations.

In your country and in mine, every businessman is persuaded that inflation is produced by labour unions, or by wage pressure, whether or not from trade unions. And that is because of the fallacy of composition. What is true for each individual is often the *opposite* of what is true for everybody together. Any person in this room could get out of that door in two seconds; but if everybody tried at once to get out of that door, you could not do it. In the same way, pressure on an employer to increase his prices comes to him in the form of an increase in wages and costs. It looks to him as if he is being required to increase prices because of that increase in wages and costs. That is true for him by himself. But where did that increase in costs come from? It came because somewhere else in the system somebody was increasing demand, which was tending to draw away the employer's labour or other resources. He was required to bid in the market to keep them.

In *University Economics*,[17] Professors A. A. Alchian and W. R. Allen have an excellent little parable which I think brings this truth home very well. It says, let us suppose in a country in which everything else is fine all of a sudden there is a great craze for increasing the consumption of meat, and all the housewives rush to the butchers to buy meat. The butchers are delighted to sell them the meat. They do not mark up the prices at all, they just sell out all the meat they have, but they place additional orders with the wholesalers. The wholesalers are delighted to sell the meat. They clean out their inventories. They go back to the packing houses. The packing houses ship out their meat. The price is the same but the packing houses send orders to their buyers at the cattle market: 'Buy more beef.' There is only a fixed amount of cattle available. And so the only thing that happens is that in the process of each packer trying to buy more beef he bids up the price. Then a notice goes from the packer to the wholesaler, 'We are very sorry, but due to an increase in our costs we are required to increase the price.' A notice goes from the wholesaler to the retailer. And the retailer finally says to the customer when she comes in to complain that beef has gone up, 'I'm terribly sorry, but my *costs* have gone up.' He's right. But what started the increase in costs all the way up and down the line? It was the *housewife* rushing in to buy the meat.

In exactly the same way, every businessman has a misconception of the process. From his point of view he is right – the pressure on him to raise his prices derives from increases in costs. If there happen to be unions, he will attribute it to the pressure of the unions. If there are no unions, he will attribute it to some other force which is driving up wages – perhaps the world shortage of sugar, or the Arabs. But the truth of the matter is that the ultimate source of inflation is always that increase in *demand* which percolates through to him in this or some other form.

Notes

1   June 1926, pp. 785–92. It was reprinted in the *Journal of Political Economy*, March/April 1973, pp. 496–502.
2   'The Relation between Unemployment and the Rate of Change of Money Wage Rates in the United Kingdom, 1861–1957', *Economica*, November 1958, pp. 283–99.
3   Fisher, *op.cit.*, p. 786.
4   *Ibid.*, p. 787.
5   *Ibid.*, p. 788.
6   Phillips, *op.cit.*, p. 283.
7   J.M. Keynes, *The General Theory of Employment, Interest, and Money* (Macmillan, 1936): 'Whilst workers will usually resist a reduction of money-wages, it is not their practice to withdraw their labour whenever there is a rise in the price of wage-goods' (p. 9). ' ... The workers, though unconsciously, are instinctively more reasonable economists than the classical school ... They resist reductions of money-wages ... whereas they do not resist reductions of real wages' (p.14). ' ... Since no trade union would dream of striking on every occasion of a rise in the cost of living, they do not raise the obstacle to any increase in aggregate employment attributed to them by the classical school' (p.15).
8   For example, Albert Rees, 'The Phillips Curve as a Menu for Policy Choices', *Economica*, August 1970, pp. 227–38, explicitly considers the objections to a stable Phillips curve outlined below, yet concludes that there remains a trade-off that should be exploited. He writes: 'The strongest policy conclusion I can draw from the expectations literature is that the policy makers should not attempt to operate at a single point on the Phillips curve ... Rather, they should permit fluctuations in the unemployment within a band' (p. 238).
9   'The Role of Monetary Policy', *American Economic Review*, March 1968, pp. 1–17.
10 'Money Wage Dynamics and Labour Market Equilibrium,' in E. S. Phelps (ed.), *Microeconomic Foundations of Employment and Inflation Theory*, Norton, New York, 1970.
11 'United Kingdom General Index of Retail Prices', *Department of Employment Gazette*.
12 This is the coefficient of the anticipated rate of inflation, that is, the percentage point change in the current rate of change in wages or in prices that would result from a 1 percentage point change in the anticipated rate of inflation.
13 I might note as an aside that one much noticed attempt along these lines was contained in lectures given in Britain by Robert Solow a few years ago (*Price Expectations and the Behaviour of the Price Level*, Manchester University Press, 1969). Unfortunately, his test has a fatal flaw which renders

it irrelevant to the current issue. In order to allow for costs as well as demand, he included on the right-hand side of an equation like equation (3) the rate of change of wages, and, on the left-hand side, the rate of change of prices. In such an equation, there is no reason to expect b to be unity even on the strictest acceleration hypothesis, because the equation is then an equation to determine what happens to the margin between prices and wages. Let the anticipated rate of inflation rise by one percentage point, but the rate of change of wages be held constant, and any resulting rise in prices raises the excess of prices over costs and so stimulates output. Hence, in Solow's equation, the strict acceleration hypothesis would imply that b was less than 1.

14 A succinct summary of these studies is in S. J. Turnovsky, 'On the Role of Inflationary Expectations in a Short-Run Macro-Economic Model', *Economic Journal*, June 1974, pp. 317–37, especially pp. 326–7.

15 John Muth, 'Rational Expectations and the Theory of Price Movements', *Econometrica*, July 1961, pp. 315–35; Robert E. Lucas, 'Econometric Testing of the Natural Rate Hypothesis', in Otto Eckstein (ed.), *The Econometrics of Price Determination Conference*, Board of Governors of the Federal Reserve System and Social Science Research Council, Washington, 1972, 'Econometric Policy Evaluation: A Critique', Carnegie–Mellon University Working Paper, 1973 and 'Some International Evidence on Output-Inflation Tradeoffs', *American Economic Review*, June 1973, pp. 326–34; Thomas J. Sargent, 'Rational Expectations, the Real Rate of Interest, and the "Natural" Rate of Unemployment', *Brookings Papers on Economic Activity* 2, 1973, pp. 429–72; and Thomas J. Sargent and Neil Wallace, '"Rational" Expectations, the Optimal Money Instrument and the Optimal Money Supply Rule', *Journal of Political Economy*, April 1974.

16 Listed in note 15 above.

17 Third edn, Wadsworth, Belmont, California, 1972; international paperback edn, with a new Introduction by A. J. Culyer, Prentice-Hall, Hemel Hempstead, Herts., 1974, pp. 95–7.

5

Inflation and Unemployment: the New Dimension of Politics

When the Bank of Sweden established the prize for Economic Science in memory of Alfred Nobel (1968), there doubtless was – as there doubtless still remains – widespread scepticism among both scientists and the broader public about the appropriateness of treating economics as parallel to physics, chemistry, and medicine. These are regarded as 'exact sciences' in which objective, cumulative, definitive knowledge is possible. Economics, and its fellow social sciences, are regarded more nearly as branches of philosophy than of science properly defined, enmeshed with values at the outset because they deal with human behaviour. Do not the social sciences, in which scholars are analysing the behaviour of themselves and their fellow men, who are in turn observing and reacting to what the scholars say, require fundamentally different methods of investigation than the physical and biological sciences? Should they not be judged by different criteria?

1 Social and Natural Sciences

I have never myself accepted this view. I believe that it reflects a misunderstanding not so much of the character and possibilities of social science as of the character and possibilities of natural science. In both, there is no 'certain' substantive knowledge; only tentative hypotheses that can never be 'proved', but can only fail to be rejected, hypotheses in which we may have more or less confidence, depending on such

The 1976 Alfred Nobel Memorial Lecture, delivered in Stockholm in December 1976; published originally as IEA Occasional Paper No. 51 (1977).

features as the breadth of experience they encompass relative to their own complexity and relative to alternative hypotheses, and the number of occasions on which they have escaped possible rejection. In both social and natural sciences, the body of positive knowledge grows by the failure of a tentative hypothesis to predict phenomena the hypothesis professes to explain; by the patching up of that hypothesis until someone suggests a new hypothesis that more elegantly or simply embodies the troublesome phenomena, and so on *ad infinitum*. In both, experiment is sometimes possible, sometimes not (witness meteorology). In both, no experiment is ever completely controlled, and experience often offers evidence that is the equivalent of controlled experiment. In both, there is no way to have a self-contained closed system or to avoid interaction between the observer and the observed. The Gödel theorem in mathematics, the Heisenberg uncertainty principle in physics, the self-fulfilling or self-defeating prophecy in the social sciences all exemplify these limitations.

Of course, the different sciences deal with different subject matter, have different bodies of evidence to draw on (for example, introspection is a more important source of evidence for social than for natural sciences), find different techniques of analysis most useful, and have achieved differential success in predicting the phenomena they are studying. But such differences are as great among, say, physics, biology, medicine, and meteorology as between any of them and economics.

Even the difficult problem of separating value-judgements from scientific judgements is not unique to the social sciences. I well recall a dinner at a Cambridge University college when I was sitting between a fellow economist and R. A. Fisher, the great mathematical statistician and geneticist. My fellow economist told me about a student he had been tutoring on labour economics, who, in connection with an analysis of the effect of trade unions, remarked, 'Well surely, Mr X (another economist of a different political persuasion) would not agree with that.' My colleague regarded this experience as a terrible indictment of economics because it illustrated the impossibility of a value-free positive economic science. I turned to Sir Ronald and asked whether such an experience was indeed unique to social science. His answer was an impassioned 'no', and he proceeded to tell one story after another about how accurately he could infer views in genetics from political views.

One of my great teachers, Wesley C. Mitchell, impressed on me the basic reason why scholars have every incentive to pursue a value-free science, whatever their values and however strongly they may wish to spread and promote them. In order to recommend a course of action to achieve an objective, we must first know whether that course of action will in fact promote the objective. Positive scientific knowledge that enables us to predict the consequences of a possible course of action is clearly a prerequisite for the normative judgement whether that course of action is desirable. The Road to Hell is paved with good intentions, precisely because of the neglect of this rather obvious point.

This point is particularly important in economics. Many countries around the world are today experiencing socially destructive inflation, abnormally high unemployment, misuse of economic resources, and in some cases, the suppression of human freedom not because evil men deliberately sought to achieve these results, nor because of differences in values among their citizens, but because of erroneous judgements about the consequences of government measures: errors that at least in principle are capable of being corrected by the progress of positive economic science.

Rather than pursue these ideas in the abstract,[1] I shall illustrate the positive scientific character of economics by discussing a particular economic issue that has been a major concern of the economics profession throughout the post-war period; namely, the relation between inflation and unemployment. This issue is an admirable illustration because it has been a controversial political issue throughout the period, yet the drastic change that has occurred in accepted professional views was produced primarily by the scientific response to experience that contradicted a tentatively accepted hypothesis – precisely the classical process for the revision of a scientific hypothesis.

I cannot give here an exhaustive survey of the work that has been done on this issue or of the evidence that has led to the revision of the hypothesis. I shall be able only to skim the surface in the hope of conveying the flavour of that work and that evidence and of indicating the major items requiring further investigation.

Professional controversy about the relation between inflation and unemployment has been intertwined with controversy about the relative rôle of monetary, fiscal, and other factors in influencing aggregate demand. One issue deals with how a change in aggregate nominal demand, however produced, works itself out through changes in employment and price levels; the other, with the factors accounting for the changes in aggregate nominal demand.

The two issues are closely related. The effects of a change in aggregate nominal demand on employment and price levels may not be independent of the source of the change, and conversely, the effect of monetary, fiscal, or other forces on aggregate nominal demand may depend on how employment and price levels react. A full analysis will clearly have to treat the two issues jointly. Yet there is a considerable measure of independence between them. To a first approximation, the effects on employment and price levels may depend only on the magnitude of the change in aggregate nominal demand, not on its source. On both issues, professional opinion today is very different than it was just after World War II because experience contradicted tentatively accepted hypotheses. Either issue could therefore serve to illustrate my main thesis. I have chosen to deal with only one in order to keep this lecture within reasonable bounds. I have chosen to make that one the relation between inflation and unemployment, because recent experience leaves me less satisfied with the adequacy of my earlier work on that issue than with the adequacy of my earlier work on the forces producing changes in aggregate nominal demand.

2 Stage I: Negatively Sloping Phillips Curve

Professional analysis of the relation between inflation and unemployment has gone through two stages since the end of World War II and is now entering a third. The first stage was the acceptance of a hypothesis associated with the name of A. W. Phillips that there is a stable negative relation between the level of unemployment and the rate of change of wages – high levels of unemployment being accompanied by falling wages, low levels of unemployment by rising wages.[2] The wage change in turn was linked to price change by allowing for the secular increase in productivity and treating the excess of price over wage cost as given by a roughly constant mark-up factor.

Figure 1 illustrates this hypothesis, where I have followed the standard practice of relating unemployment directly to price change, short-circuiting the intermediate step through wages.

This relation was widely interpreted as a causal relation that offered a stable trade-off to policy-makers. They could choose a low unemployment target, such as U_L. In that case they would have to accept an inflation rate of A. There would remain the problem of choosing the measures (monetary, fiscal, perhaps other) that would produce the level of aggregate nominal demand required to achieve U_L, but if that were done, there need be no concern about maintaining that combination of unemployment and inflation. Alternatively, the policy-makers could choose a low inflation rate or even deflation as their target. In that case

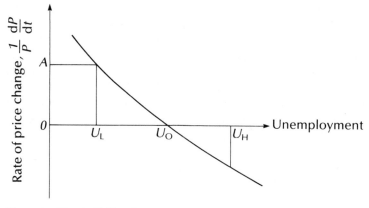

Figure 1   *Simple Phillips Curve.*

they would have to reconcile themselves to higher unemployment: U_0 for zero inflation, U_H for deflation.

Economists then busied themselves with trying to extract the relation depicted in figure 1 from evidence for different countries and periods, to eliminate the effect of extraneous disturbances, to clarify the relation between wage change and price change, and so on. In addition, they explored social gains and losses from inflation on the one hand and unemployment on the other, in order to facilitate the choice of the 'right' trade-off.

Unfortunately for this hypothesis, additional evidence failed to conform to it. Empirical estimates of the Phillips curve relation were unsatisfactory. More important, the inflation rate that appeared to be consistent with a specified level of unemployment did not remain fixed: in the circumstances of the post-World War II period, when governments everywhere were seeking to promote 'full employment', it tended in any one country to rise over time and to vary sharply among countries. Looked at the other way, rates of inflation that had earlier been associated with low levels of unemployment were experienced along with high levels of unemployment. The phenomenon of simultaneous high inflation and high unemployment increasingly forced itself on public and professional notice, receiving the unlovely label of 'stagflation'.

Some of us were sceptical from the outset about the validity of a stable Phillips curve, primarily on theoretical rather than empirical grounds.[3] What mattered for employment, we argued, was not wages in dollars or pounds or kronor but real wages – what the wages would buy in goods and services. Low unemployment would, indeed, mean pressure for a higher real wage – but real wages could be higher even if nominal wages were lower, provided that prices were still lower. Similarly, high unemployment would, indeed, mean pressure for a lower real wage – but real wages could be lower, even if nominal wages were higher, provided prices were still higher.

There is no need to assume a stable Phillips curve in order to explain the apparent tendency for an acceleration of inflation to reduce unemployment. That can be explained by the impact of *unanticipated* changes in nominal demand on markets characterised by (implicit or explicit) long-term commitments with respect to both capital and labour. Long-term labour commitments can be explained by the cost of acquiring information by employers about employees and by employees about alternative employment opportunities plus the specific human capital that makes an employee's value to a particular employer grow over time and exceed his value to other potential employers.

Only surprises matter. If everyone anticipated that prices would rise at, say, 20 per cent a year, then this anticipation would be embodied in future wage (and other) contracts, real wages would then behave precisely as they would if everyone anticipated no price rise, and there would be no reason for the 20 per cent rate of inflation to be associated with a different level of unemployment than a zero rate. An unanticipated change is very different, especially in the presence of long-term commitments – themselves partly a result of the imperfect knowledge whose effect they enhance and spread over time. Long-term commitments mean, first, that there is not instantaneous market clearing (as in markets for perishable foods) but only a lagged adjustment of both prices and quantity to changes in demand or supply (as in the house-rental market); second, that commitments entered into depend not only on current observable prices, but also on the prices expected to prevail throughout the term of the commitment.

3 Stage 2: the Natural Rate Hypothesis

Proceeding along these lines, we[4] developed an alternative hypothesis that distinguished between the short-run and long-run effects of unanticipated changes in aggregate nominal demand. Start from some initial stable position and let there be, for example, an unanticipated acceleration of aggregate nominal demand. This will come to each producer as an unexpectedly favourable demand for his product. In an environment in which changes are always occurring in the relative demand for different goods, he will not know whether this change is special to him or pervasive. It will be rational for him to interpret it as at least partly special and to react to it, by seeking to produce more to sell at what he now perceives to be a higher than expected market price for future output. He will be willing to pay higher nominal wages than he had been willing to pay before in order to attract additional workers. The real wage that matters to him is the wage in terms of the price of his product, and he perceives that price is higher than before. A higher nominal wage can therefore mean a lower *real* wage as perceived by him.

To workers, the situation is different: what matters to them is the purchasing power of wages not over the particular good they produce but over all goods in general. Both they and their employers are likely to adjust more slowly their perception of prices in general – because it is more costly to acquire information about that – than their perception of the price of the particular good they produce. As a result, a rise in nominal wages may be perceived by workers as a rise in real wages and hence call forth an increased supply, at the same time that it is perceived by employers as a fall in real wages and hence calls forth an increased offer of jobs. Expressed in terms of the average of perceived future prices, real wages are lower; in terms of the perceived future average price, real wages are higher.

But this situation is temporary: let the higher rate of growth of aggregate nominal demand and of prices continue, and perceptions will adjust to reality. When they do, the initial effect will disappear, and then even be reversed for a time as workers and employers find themselves locked into inappropriate contracts. Ultimately, employment will be back at the level that prevailed before the assumed unanticipated acceleration in aggregate nominal demand.

This alternative hypothesis is depicted in figure 2. Each negatively sloping curve is a Phillips curve like that in figure 1 except that it is for a particular anticipated or perceived rate of inflation, defined as the perceived average rate of price change, *not* the average of perceived rates

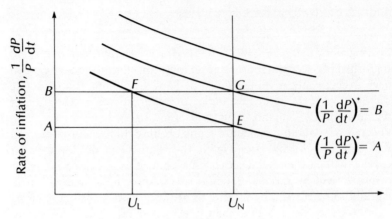

Figure 2   *Expectations-adjusted Phillips Curve.*

of individual price change (the order of the curves would be reversed for the second concept). Start from point E and let the rate of inflation for whatever reason move from A to B and stay there. Unemployment would initially decline to U_L at point F, moving along the curve defined for an anticipated rate of inflation

$$\left(\frac{1}{P} \frac{dP}{dt} \right)^*$$

of A. As anticipations adjusted, the short-run curve would move upward, ultimately to the curve defined for an anticipated inflation rate of B. Concurrently unemployment would move gradually over from F to G.[5]

This analysis is, of course, over-simplified. It supposes a single unanticipated change, whereas, of course, there is a continuing stream of unanticipated changes; it does not deal explicitly with lags, or with overshooting; or with the process of formation of anticipations. But it does highlight the key points: what matters is not inflation *per se*, but unanticipated inflation; there is no stable trade-off between inflation and unemployment; there is a 'natural rate of unemployment' (U_N), which is consistent with the real forces and with accurate perceptions; unemployment can be kept below that level only by an accelerating inflation; or above it, only by accelerating deflation.

The 'natural rate of unemployment', a term I introduced to parallel Knut Wicksell's 'natural rate of interest', is not a numerical constant but depends on 'real' as opposed to monetary factors – the effectiveness of the labour market, the extent of competition or monopoly, the barriers or encouragements to working in various occupations, and so on.

For example, the natural rate has clearly been rising in the United States for two major reasons. First, women, teenagers, and part-time workers have been constituting a growing fraction of the labour force. These groups are more mobile in employment than other workers, entering and leaving the labour market, shifting more frequently between jobs. As a result, they tend to experience higher average rates of unemployment. Second, unemployment insurance and other forms of assistance to unemployed persons have been made available to more categories of workers, and have become more generous in duration and amount. Workers who lose their jobs are under less pressure to look for other work, will tend to wait longer in the hope, generally fulfilled, of being recalled to their former employment, and can be more selective in the alternatives they consider. Further, the availability of unemployment insurance makes it more attractive to enter the labour force in the first place, and so may itself have stimulated the growth that has occurred in the labour force as a percentage of the population and also its changing composition.

The determinants of the natural rate of unemployment deserve much fuller analysis for both the United States and other countries. So also do the meaning of the recorded unemployment figures and the relation between the recorded figures and the natural rate. These issues are all of the utmost importance for public policy. However, they are side issues for my present limited purpose.

The connection between the state of employment and the level of efficiency or productivity of an economy is another topic that is of fundamental importance for public policy but is a side issue for my present purpose. There is a tendency to take it for granted that a high level of recorded unemployment is evidence of inefficient use of resources, and conversely. This view is seriously in error. A low level of unemployment may be a sign of a forced-draft economy that is using its resources inefficiently and is inducing workers to sacrifice leisure for goods that they value less highly than the leisure under the mistaken belief that their real wages will be higher than they prove to be. Or a low natural rate of unemployment may reflect institutional arrangements that inhibit change. A highly static rigid economy may have a fixed place for everyone whereas a dynamic, highly progressive economy, which offers ever-changing opportunities and fosters flexibility, may have a high natural rate of unemployment. To illustrate how the same rate may correspond to very different conditions: both Japan and the United Kingdom had low average rates of unemployment from, say, 1950 to 1970, but Japan experienced rapid growth, the UK, stagnation.

The 'natural-rate' or 'accelerationist' or 'expectations-adjusted Phillips curve' hypothesis – as it has been variously designated – is by now widely accepted by economists, though by no means universally. A few still cling to the original Phillips curve; more recognise the difference between short-run and long-run curves but regard even the long-run curve as negatively sloped, though more steeply so than the short-run curves; some substitute a stable relation between the acceleration of inflation and unemployment for a stable relation between inflation and unemployment – aware of, but not concerned about, the possibility that the same logic that drove them to a second derivative will drive them to ever higher derivatives.

Much current economic research is devoted to exploring various aspects of this second stage – the dynamics of the process, the formation of expectations, and the kind of systematic policy, if any, that can have a predictable effect on real magnitudes. We can expect rapid progress on these issues. (Special mention should be made of the work on 'rational expectations', especially the seminal contributions of John Muth, Robert Lucas, and Thomas Sargent.)[6]

4 Stage 3: a Positively Sloped Phillips Curve?

Although the second stage is far from having been fully explored, let alone fully absorbed into the economic literature, the course of events is already producing a move to a third stage. In recent years, higher inflation has often been accompanied by higher not lower unemployment, especially for periods of several years in length. A simple statistical Phillips curve for such periods seems to be positively sloped, not vertical. The third stage is directed at accommodating this apparent empirical phenomenon. To do so, I suspect that it will have to include in the analysis the interdependence of economic experience and political developments. It will have to treat at least some political phenomena not as independent variables – as exogenous variables in econometric jargon – but as themselves determined by economic events – as endogenous variables.[7] The second stage was greatly influenced by two major developments in economic theory of the past few decades – one, the analysis of imperfect information and of the cost of acquiring information, pioneered by George Stigler; the other, the rôle of human capital in determining the form of labour contracts, pioneered by Gary Becker. The third stage will, I believe, be greatly influenced by a third major development – the application of economic analysis to political behaviour, a field in which pioneering work has also been done by Stigler and Becker as well as by Kenneth Arrow, Duncan Black, Anthony Downs, James Buchanan, Gordon Tullock, and others.

The apparent positive relation between inflation and unemployment has been a source of great concern to government policy-makers. Let me quote from a recent speech by Prime Minister Callaghan of Great Britain:

> We used to think that you could spend your way out of a recession, and increase employment by cutting taxes and boosting Government spending. I tell you, in all candour, that that option no longer exists, and that, insofar as it ever did exist, it only worked by ... injecting bigger doses of inflation into the economy, followed by higher levels of unemployment as the next step ..... That is the history of the past 20 years.[8]

The same view is expressed in a Canadian Government white paper:

> Continuing inflation, particularly in North America, has been accompanied by an increase in measured unemployment rates.[9]

These are remarkable statements, running as they do directly counter to the policies adopted by almost every Western government throughout the post-war period.

(a) Some evidence

More systematic evidence for the past two decades is given in table 1 and figures 3 and 4, which show the rates of inflation and unemployment in seven industrialised countries over the past two decades. According to the five-year averages in table 1, the rate of inflation and the level of unemployment moved in opposite directions – the expected simple Phillips curve outcome – in five out of seven countries between the first two quinquennia (1956–60, 1961–65); in only four out of seven countries between the second and third quinquennia (1961–65 and 1966–70); and in only one of seven countries between the final two quinquennia (1966–70 and 1970–75). And even the one exception – Italy – is not a real

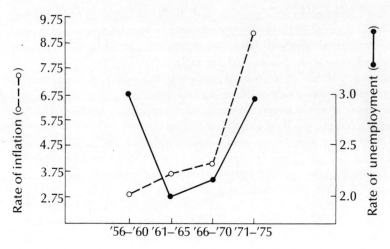

Figure 3   *Rates of unemployment and inflation, 1956–75, by quinquennia: unweighted average for seven countries.*

exception. True, unemployment averaged a shade lower from 1971 to 1975 than in the prior five years, despite a more than tripling of the rate of inflation. However, since 1973, both inflation and unemployment have risen sharply.

The averages for all seven countries plotted in figure 3 bring out even more clearly the shift from a negatively sloped simple Phillips curve to a positively sloped one. The two curves move in opposite directions between the first two quinquennia; in the same direction thereafter.

The annual data in figure 4 tell a similar, though more confused, story. In the early years, there is wide variation in the relation between prices and unemployment, varying from essentially no relation, as in Italy, to a fairly clear-cut year-to-year negative relation, as in the UK and the US. In recent years, however, France, the US, the UK, Germany and Japan all show a clearly marked rise in both inflation and unemployment – though for Japan, the rise in unemployment is much smaller relative to the rise in inflation than in the other countries, reflecting the different meaning of unemployment in the different institutional environment of Japan. Only Sweden and Italy fail to conform to the general pattern.

Of course, these data are at most suggestive. We do not really have seven independent bodies of data. Common international influences affect all countries so that multiplying the number of countries does not multiply proportionately the amount of evidence. In particular, the oil

TABLE 1 Inflation and unemployment in seven countries, 1956–75: average values for successive quinquennia. DP = rate of price change, per cent, per year; U = unemployment, percentage of labour force

	France		Germany		Italy		Japan		Sweden		United Kingdom		United States		Unweighted average	
	DP	U	DP	U	DP	U	DP	U	DP	U	DP	U	DP	U	DP	U
1956–60	5.6	1.1	1.8	2.9	1.9	6.7	1.9	1.4	3.7	1.9	2.6	1.5	2.0	5.2	2.8	3.0
1961–5	3.7	1.2	2.8	0.7	4.9	3.1	6.2	0.9	3.6	1.2	3.5	1.6	1.3	5.5	3.7	2.0
1966–70	4.4	1.7	2.4	1.2	3.0	3.5	5.4	1.1	4.6	1.6	4.6	2.1	4.2	3.9	4.1	2.2
1971–5	8.8	2.5	6.1	2.1	11.3	3.3	11.4	1.4	7.9	1.8	13.0	3.2	6.7	6.1	9.3	2.9

Note: DP is rate of change of consumer prices compounded annually from calendar year 1955 to 1960; 1960 to 1965; 1965 to 1970; 1970 to 1975. U is average unemployment during five indicated calendar years). As a result, DP is dated one-half year prior to associated U.

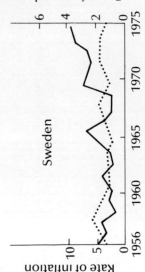

Rate of inflation
Rate of unemployment

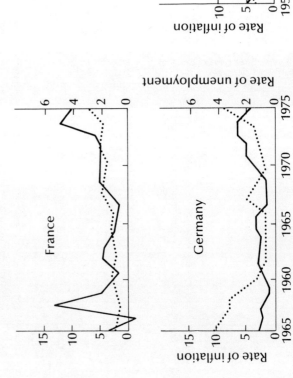

France

Germany

Sweden

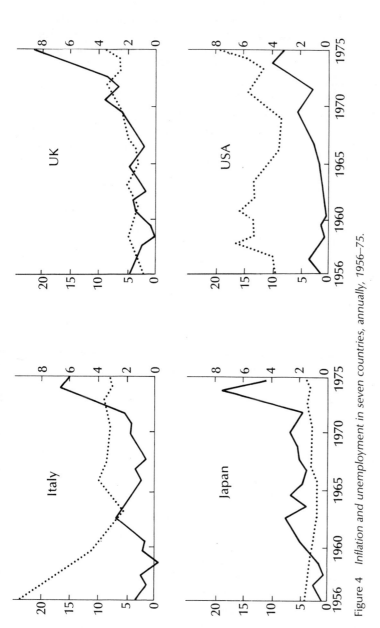

Figure 4 *Inflation and unemployment in seven countries, annually, 1956–75.*

crisis hit all seven countries at the same time. Whatever effect the crisis had on the rate of inflation, it directly disrupted the productive process and tended to increase unemployment. Any such increases can hardly be attributed to the acceleration of inflation that accompanied them; at most the two could be regarded as at least partly the common result of a third influence.[10]

Both the quinquennial and annual data show that the oil crisis cannot wholly explain the phenomenon described so graphically by Mr Callaghan. Already before the quadrupling of oil prices in 1973, most countries show a clearly marked association of rising inflation and rising unemployment. But this too may reflect independent forces rather than the influence of inflation on unemployment. For example, the same forces that have been raising the natural rate of unemployment in the US may have been operating in other countries and may account for their rising trend of unemployment, independently of the consequences of inflation.

Despite these qualifications, the data strongly suggest that, at least in some countries, of which Britain, Canada, and Italy may be the best examples, rising inflation and rising unemployment have been mutually reinforcing, rather than the separate effects of separate causes. The data are not inconsistent with the stronger statement that, in all industrialised countries, higher rates of inflation have some effects that, at least for a time, make for higher unemployment. The rest of this paper is devoted to a preliminary exploration of what some of these effects may be.

(b) A tentative hypothesis

I conjecture that a modest elaboration of the natural-rate hypothesis is all that is required to account for a positive relation between inflation and unemployment, though of course such a positive relation may also occur for other reasons. Just as the natural-rate hypothesis explains a negatively sloped Phillips curve over short periods as a temporary phenomenon that will disappear as economic agents adjust their expectations to reality, so a positively sloped Phillips curve over somewhat longer periods may occur as a transitional phenomenon that will disappear as economic agents adjust not only their expectations but their institutional and political arrangements to a new reality. When this is achieved, I believe that – as the natural-rate hypothesis suggests – the rate of unemployment will be largely independent of the average rate of inflation, though the efficiency of utilisation of resources may not be. High inflation need not mean either abnormally high or abnormally low unemployment. However, the institutional and political arrangements that accompany it, either as relics of earlier history or as products of the inflation itself, are likely to prove antithetical to the most productive use of employed resources – a special case of the distinction between the state of employment and the productivity of an economy referred to earlier.

Experience in many Latin American countries that have adjusted to chronically high inflation rates – experience that has been analysed most perceptively by some of my colleagues, particularly Arnold Harberger and Larry Sjaastad[11] – is consistent, I believe, with this view.

In the version of the natural-rate hypothesis summarised in figure 2, the vertical curve is for alternative rates of fully anticipated inflation. Whatever that rate – be it negative, zero, or positive – it can be built into every decision if it is fully anticipated. At an anticipated 20 per cent per year inflation, for example, long-term wage contracts would provide for a wage in each year that would rise relative to the zero-inflation wage by just 20 per cent per year; long-term loans would bear an interest rate 20 percentage points higher than the zero-inflation rate, or a principal that would be raised by 20 per cent a year; and so on – in short, the equivalent of a full indexing of all contracts. The high rate of inflation would have some real effects, by altering desired cash balances, for example, but it need not alter the efficiency of labour markets, or the length or terms of labour contracts, and hence, it need not change the natural rate of unemployment.

This analysis implicitly supposes, first, that inflation is steady or at least no more variable at a high rate than at a low – otherwise, it is unlikely that inflation would be as fully anticipated at high as at low rates of inflation; second, that the inflation is, or can be, open, with all prices free to adjust to the higher rate, so that relative price adjustments are the same with a 20 per cent inflation as with a zero inflation; third, really a variant of the second point, that there are no obstacles to indexing of contracts.

Ultimately, if inflation at an average rate of 20 per cent per year were to prevail for many decades, these requirements could come fairly close to being met, which is why I am inclined to retain the long-long-run vertical Phillips curve. But when a country initially moves to higher rates of inflation, these requirements will be systematically departed from. And such a transitional period may well extend over decades.

Consider, in particular, the US and the UK. For two centuries before World War II for the UK, and a century and a half for the US, prices varied about a roughly constant level, showing substantial increases in time of war, then post-war declines to roughly pre-war levels. The concept of a 'normal' price level was deeply embedded in the financial and other institutions of the two countries and in the habits and attitudes of their citizens.

In the immediate post-World War II period, prior experience was widely expected to recur. The fact was post-war inflation superimposed on wartime inflation; yet the expectation in both the US and the UK was deflation. It took a long time for the fear of post-war deflation to dissipate – if it still has – and still longer before expectations started to adjust to the fundamental change in the monetary system. That adjustment is still far from complete.[12]

Indeed, we do not know what a complete adjustment will consist of. We cannot know now whether the industrialised countries will return to the pre-World War II pattern of a long-term stable price level, or will move towards the Latin American pattern of chronically high inflation rates – with every now and then an acute outbreak of super- or hyper-inflation, as occurred recently in Chile and Argentina[13] – or will undergo more radical economic and political change leading to a still different resolution of the present ambiguous situation.

This uncertainty – or more precisely, the circumstances producing this uncertainty – leads to systematic departures from the conditions required for a vertical Phillips curve.

The most fundamental departure is that a high inflation rate is not likely to be steady during the transition decades. Rather, the higher the rate, the more variable it is likely to be. That has been empirically true of differences among countries in the past several decades.[14] It is also highly plausible on theoretical grounds – both about actual inflation and, even more clearly, the anticipations of economic agents with respect to inflation. Governments have not produced high inflation as a deliberate announced policy but as a consequence of other policies – in particular, policies of full employment and welfare state policies raising government spending. They all proclaim their adherence to the goal of stable prices. They do so in response to their constituents, who may welcome many of the side-effects of inflation, but are still wedded to the concept of stable money. A burst of inflation produces strong pressure to counter it. Policy goes from one direction to the other, encouraging wide variation in the actual and anticipated rate of inflation. And, of course, in such an environment, no one has single-valued anticipations. Everyone recognises that there is great uncertainty about what actual inflation will turn out to be over any specific future interval.[15]

The tendency for inflation that is high on the average to be highly

variable is reinforced by the effect of inflation on the political cohes-
iveness of a country in which institutional arrangements and financial
contracts have been adjusted to a long-term 'normal' price level. Some
groups gain (e.g. home owners); others lose (e.g. owners of savings
accounts and fixed interest securities). 'Prudent' behaviour becomes in
fact reckless, and 'reckless' behaviour in fact prudent. The society is
polarised; one group is set against another. Political unrest increases.
The capacity of any government to govern is reduced at the same time
that the pressure for strong action grows.

An increased variability of actual or anticipated inflation may raise
the natural rate of unemployment in two rather different ways.

First, increased volatility shortens the optimum length of unindexed
commitments and renders indexing more advantageous.[16] But it takes
time for actual practice to adjust. In the meantime, prior arrangements
introduce rigidities that reduce the effectiveness of markets. An additional
element of uncertainty is, as it were, added to every market arrangement.
In addition, indexing is, even at best, an imperfect substitute for stability
of the inflation rate. Price indexes are imperfect; they are available only
with a lag, and generally are applied to contract terms only with a further
lag.

These developments clearly lower economic efficiency. It is less clear
what their effect is on recorded unemployment. High average inventories
of all kinds is one way to meet increased rigidity and uncertainty. But
that may mean labour-hoarding by enterprises and low unemployment
or a larger force of workers between jobs and so high unemployment.
Shorter commitments may mean more rapid adjustment of employment
to changed conditions and so low unemployment, or the delay in adjusting the length of commitments may lead to less satisfactory adjustment
and so high unemployment. Clearly, much additional research is necessary in this area to clarify the relative importance of the various effects.
About all one can say now is that the slow adjustment of commitments
and the imperfections of indexing may contribute to the recorded increase
in unemployment.

A second related effect of increased volatility of inflation is to render
market prices a less efficient system for co-ordinating economic activity.
A fundamental function of a price system, as Hayek[17] emphasised so
brilliantly, is to transmit compactly, efficiently, and at low cost the
information that economic agents need in order to decide what to
produce and how to produce it, or how to employ owned resources. The
relevant information is about *relative* prices – of one product relative to
another, of the services of one factor of production relative to another,

of products relative to factor services, of prices now relative to prices in the future. But the information in practice is transmitted in the form of *absolute* prices – prices in dollars or pounds or kronor. If the price level is on the average stable or changing at a steady rate, it is relatively easy to extract the signal about relative prices from the observed absolute prices. The more volatile the rate of general inflation, the harder it becomes to extract the signal about relative prices from the absolute prices: the broadcast about relative prices is as it were being jammed by the noise coming from the inflation broadcast.[18] At the extreme, the system of absolute prices becomes nearly useless, and economic agents resort either to an alternative currency, or to barter, with disastrous effects on productivity.

Again, the effect on economic efficiency is clear, on unemployment less so. But, again, it seems plausible that the average level of unemployment would be raised by the increased amount of noise in market signals, at least during the period when institutional arrangements are not yet adapted to the new situation.

These effects of increased volatility of inflation would occur even if prices were legally free to adjust – if, in that sense, the inflation were open. In practice, the distorting effects of uncertainty, rigidity of voluntary long-term contracts, and the contamination of price signals will almost certainly be reinforced by legal restrictions on price change. In the modern world, governments are themselves producers of services sold on the market: from postal services to a wide range of other items. Other prices are regulated by government, and require government approval for change: from air fares to taxicab fares to charges for electricity. In these cases, governments cannot avoid being involved in the price-fixing process. In addition, the social and political forces unleashed by volatile inflation rates will lead governments to try to repress inflation in still other areas: by explicit price and wage control, or by pressuring private businesses or unions 'voluntarily' to exercise 'restraint', or by speculating in foreign exchange in order to alter the exchange rate.

The details will vary from time to time and from country to country, but the general result is the same: reduction in the capacity of the price system to guide economic activity; distortions in relative prices because of the introduction of greater friction, as it were, in all markets; and, very likely, a higher recorded rate of unemployment.[19]

The forces I have just described may render the political and economic system dynamically unstable and produce hyper-inflation and radical political change – as in many defeated countries after World War I, or in Chile and Argentina more recently. At the other extreme, before any such catastrophe occurs, policies may be adopted that will achieve a relatively low and stable rate of inflation and lead to the dismantling of many of the interferences with the price system. That would re-establish the preconditions for the straightforward natural-rate hypothesis and enable that hypothesis to be used to predict the course of the transition.

. An intermediate possibility is that the system will reach stability at a fairly constant though high average rate of inflation. In that case, unemployment should also settle down to a fairly constant level decidedly lower than during the transition. As the preceding discussion emphasises, *increasing* volatility and *increasing* government intervention with the price system are the major factors that seem likely to raise unemployment, not *high* volatility or a *high* level of intervention.

Ways of coping with both volatility and intervention will develop: through indexing and similar arrangements for coping with volatility of inflation; through the development of indirect ways of altering prices and wages for avoiding government controls.

Under these circumstances, the long-run Phillips curve would again be vertical, and we would be back at the natural-rate hypothesis, though perhaps for a different range of inflation rates than that for which it was first suggested.

Because the phenomenon to be explained is the co-existence of high inflation and high unemployment, I have stressed the effect of institutional changes produced by a transition from a monetary system in which there was a 'normal' price level to a monetary system consistent with long periods of high, and possibly highly variable, inflation. It should be noted that, once these institutional changes were made, and economic agents had adjusted their practices and anticipations to them, a reversal to the earlier monetary framework or even the adoption in the new monetary framework of a successful policy of low inflation would in its turn require new adjustments, and these might have many of the same adverse transitional effects on the level of employment. There would appear to be an intermediate-run negatively sloped Phillips curve instead of the positively sloped one I have tried to rationalise.

5 Conclusion

One consequence of the Keynesian revolution of the 1930s was the acceptance of a rigid absolute wage level, and a nearly rigid absolute price level, as a starting point for analysing short-term economic change. It came to be taken for granted that these were essentially institutional data and were so regarded by economic agents, so that changes in aggregate nominal demand would be reflected almost entirely in output and hardly at all in prices. The age-old confusion between absolute prices and relative prices gained a new lease of life.

In this intellectual atmosphere it was understandable that economists would analyse the relation between unemployment and *nominal* rather than *real* wages and would implicitly regard changes in anticipated *nominal* wages as equal to changes in anticipated *real* wages. Moreover, the empirical evidence that initially suggested a stable relation between the level of unemployment and the rate of change of nominal wages was drawn from a period when, despite sharp short-period fluctuations in prices, there was a relatively stable long-run price level and when the expectation of continued stability was widely shared. Hence these data flashed no warning signals about the special character of the assumptions.

The hypothesis that there is a stable relation between the level of unemployment and the rate of inflation was adopted by the economics profession with alacrity. It filled a gap in Keynes's theoretical structure. It seemed to be the 'one equation' that Keynes himself had said 'we are ... short'.[20] In addition, it seemed to provide a reliable tool for economic policy, enabling the economist to inform the policy-maker about the alternatives available to him.

As in any science, so long as experience seemed to be consistent with the reigning hypothesis, it continued to be accepted, although, as always, a few dissenters questioned its validity.

But as the 1950s turned into the 1960s, and the 1960s into the 1970s, it became increasingly difficult to accept the hypothesis in its simple form. It seemed to take larger and larger doses of inflation to keep down the level of unemployment. Stagflation reared its ugly head.

Many attempts were made to patch up the hypothesis by allowing for special factors such as the strength of trade unions. But experience stubbornly refused to conform to the patched-up version.

A more radical revision was required. It took the form of stressing the importance of surprises – of differences between actual and anticipated magnitudes. It restored the primacy of the distinction between 'real' and 'nominal' magnitudes. There is a 'natural rate of unemployment' at any time determined by real factors. This natural rate will tend to be attained when expectations are on the average realised. The same real situation is consistent with any absolute level of prices or of price change, provided allowance is made for the effect of price change on the real cost of holding money balances. In this respect, money is neutral. On the other hand, unanticipated changes in aggregate nominal demand and in inflation will cause systematic errors of perception on the part of employers and employees alike that will initially lead unemployment to deviate in the opposite direction from its natural rate. In this respect, money is not neutral. However, such deviations are transitory, though it may take a long chronological time before they are reversed and finally eliminated as anticipations adjust.

The natural-rate hypothesis contains the original Phillips curve hypothesis as a special case and rationalises a far broader range of experience, in particular the phenomenon of stagflation. It has by now been widely though not universally accepted.

However, the natural-rate hypothesis in its present form has not proved rich enough to explain a more recent development – a move from stagflation to slumpflation. In recent years, higher inflation has often been accompanied by higher unemployment – not lower unemployment, as the simple Phillips curve would suggest, nor the same unemployment, as the natural-rate hypothesis would suggest.

This recent association of higher inflation with higher unemployment may reflect the common impact of such events as the oil crisis, or independent forces that have imparted a common upward trend to inflation and unemployment.

However, a major factor in some countries and a contributing factor in others may be that they are in a transitional period – this time to be measured by quinquennia or decades, not years. The public has not adapted its attitudes or its institutions to a new monetary environment. Inflation tends not only to be higher but also increasingly volatile and to be accompanied by widening government intervention into the setting of prices. The growing volatility of inflation and the growing departure of relative prices from the values that market forces alone would set combine to render the economic system less efficient, to introduce frictions in all markets, and, very likely, to raise the recorded rate of unemployment.

On this analysis, the present situation cannot last. It will either degenerate into hyper-inflation and radical change; or institutions will adjust to a situation of chronic inflation; or governments will adopt policies that will produce a low rate of inflation and less government intervention into the fixing of prices.

I have told a perfectly standard story of how scientific theories are revised. Yet it is a story that has far-reaching importance.

Government policy about inflation and unemployment has been at the centre of political controversy. Ideological war has raged over these matters. Yet the drastic change that has occurred in economic theory has not been a result of ideological warfare. It has not resulted from divergent political beliefs or aims. It has responded almost entirely to the force of events: brute experience proved far more potent than the strongest of political or ideological preferences.

The importance for humanity of a correct understanding of positive economic science is vividly brought out by a statement made nearly two hundred years ago by Pierre S. du Pont, a Deputy from Nemours to the French National Assembly, speaking, appropriately enough, on the proposal to issue additional *assignats* – the fiat money of the French Revolution:

> Gentlemen, it is a disagreeable custom to which one is too easily led by the harshness of the discussions, to assume evil intentions. It is necessary to be gracious as to intentions; one should believe them good, and apparently they are; but we do not have to be gracious at all to inconsistent logic or to absurd reasoning. Bad logicians have committed more involuntary crimes than bad men have done intentionally. (25 September 1790)

Notes

1   I have discussed these methodological issues more fully in Milton Friedman, 'The Methodology of Positive Economics', *Essays in Positive Economics*, University of Chicago Press, Chicago, 1953.
2   A. W. Phillips, 'The Relationship between Unemployment and the Rate of Change of Money Wage Rates in the United Kingdom, 1861–1957', *Economica*, November 1958, pp. 283–99.
3   See Milton Friedman, 'What Price Guideposts?', in G. P. Schultz and R. Z. Aliber (eds.), *Guidelines: Informal Contracts and the Market Place*, University of Chicago Press, Chicago, 1966, pp. 17–39 and 55–61; 'An Inflationary Recession', *Newsweek*, 17 October 1966; 'The Role of Monetary Policy', *American Economic Review* 58, March 1968, pp. 1–17.
4   In particular, E. S. Phelps and myself: see Milton Friedman, 'The Role of Monetary Policy', *op. cit.*; E. S. Phelps, 'Phillips Curve, Expectations of Inflation and Optimal Unemployment Over Time', *Economica* 34, August 1967, pp. 254–81; E. S. Phelps, 'Money Wage Dynamics and Labour Market Equilibrium', in E. S. Phelps (ed.), *Microeconomic Foundations of Employment and Inflation Theory*, Norton, New York, 1970.
5   For a fuller discussion, see Milton Friedman, *Price Theory*, Aldine, Chicago, 1976, ch. 12.

6   Robert J. Gordon, 'Recent Developments in the Theory of Inflation and Unemployment', *Journal of Monetary Economics* 2, 1976, pp. 185–219.

7   Robert J. Gordon, 'The Demand and Supply of Inflation', *Journal of Law and Economics* 18, December 1975, pp. 807–36.

8   Speech to the Labour Party Conference, 28 September 1976.

9   'The Way Ahead: A Framework for Discussion', Government of Canada Working Paper, October 1976.

10   Robert J. Gordon, 'Alternative Responses of Policy to External Supply Shocks', *Brookings Papers on Economic Activity*, No. 1, 1975, pp. 183–206.

11   See Arnold C. Harberger, 'The Inflation Problem in Latin America', a report prepared for the Buenos Aires (March 1966) meeting of the InterAmerican Committee of the Alliance for Progress, published in Spanish as 'El problema de la inflación en América Latina', in Centro de Estudios Monetaris Latinoamericanos, *Boletin Mensual*, June 1966, pp. 253–69 (reprinted in Economic Development Institute, *Trabajossobre desarrollo económico*, IBRD, Washington DC, 1967); and Larry A. Sjaastad, 'Monetary Policy and Suppressed Inflation in Latin America', in R. Z. Aliber (ed.), *National Monetary Policies and the International Financial System*, University of Chicago Press, Chicago, 1974, pp. 127–38.

12   Benjamin Klein, 'Our New Monetary Standard: The Measurement and Effects of Price Uncertainty, 1880–1973', *Economic Inquiry*, December 1975, pp. 461–83.

13   Arnold C. Harberger, 'Inflation', *The Great Ideas Today, 1976*, Encyclopaedia Brittanica, Inc., Chicago, 1976, pp. 95–106.

14   Dwight Jaffe and Ephraim Kleiman, 'The Welfare Implications of Uneven Inflation', Seminar paper No.50, Institute for International Economic Studies, University of Stockholm, November 1975; Dennis E. Logue and Thomas D. Willett, 'A Note on the Relation between the Rate and Variability of Inflation', *Economica*, May 1976, pp. 151–8.

15   See Jaffe and Kleiman, *op. cit.*; David Meiselman, 'Capital Formation, Monetary and Financial Adjustments', *Proceedings*, 27th National Conference of Tax Foundation, 1976, pp. 9–15.

16   Jo Anna Gray, 'Essays on Wage Indexation', unpublished Ph.D. dissertation, University of Chicago, 1976.

17   F. A. Hayek, 'The Use of Knowledge in Society', *American Economic Review* 35, September 1945, pp. 519–30.

18   See Robert E. Lucas, 'Some International Evidence on Output – Inflation Tradeoffs', *American Economic Review* 63, June 1973, pp. 326–34; 'An Equilibrium Model of the Business Cycle', *Journal of Political Economy* 83, December 1975, pp. 1,113–44. See also Arnold C. Harberger, 'Inflation', *op. cit.*

19   Milton Friedman, *Price Theory, op. cit.*

20   J. M. Keynes, *The General Theory of Employment, Interest, and Money*, Macmillan, London, 1936, p. 276.

6

Inflation, Taxation, Indexation

We are economists. We believe that the market operates, and that the market operates no less in the political sphere than it does in the economic sphere. We have bad economic policies because that is what the market wants to buy; that is where the profit is. We have bad economic advice provided to our political authorities because that is where the market is, because there is a demand for such advice and some people will arise to meet that demand.

Our big problem in getting the right ideas across is in part a marketing problem. We have to create a demand for those right ideas. On the subject of indexing, I think it is important to distinguish between indexing which should be legislated and compulsory and indexing which should be encouraged and voluntary. I believe that taxation should be compulsorily indexed in order to improve the political institutions under which we operate.

1 Taxation Without Representation

In a way the argument for indexing both taxes and government borrowing has only an incidental relation to the present problem of inflation. Its fundamental purpose, in my opinion, is to improve our political institutions. As I have repeatedly said, inflation is a form of taxation without representation. It is the kind of tax that can be imposed without being legislated by the authorities and without having to employ

Published originally as a contribution to IEA Readings No. 14, *Inflation: Causes, Consequences, Cures* (1974).

additional tax collectors. In making that statement for this more sophisticated audience I have to distinguish various components of inflation.
The direct inflation tax is a tax on cash balances. If prices rise by 10 per
cent per year, people have to collect more of these pieces of paper that
are labelled pounds in order to keep the purchasing power of their cash
balances constant. And those extra pieces of paper are the equivalent of
vouchers certifying to the payment of a tax.

That part of the tax imposed by inflation will not be affected one way
or the other by indexing. But there are two other components of the
inflation tax. One component is that if personal and corporate income
taxes are levied in nominal terms, in terms of pounds or dollars, inflation
makes the effective rate of tax higher than it otherwise would be. I do
not know what the numerical values are here, but roughly in the United
States if personal incomes rise by 10 per cent because of an inflationary
rise in prices of 10 per cent, so that in real terms incomes stay the same,
personal taxes on the average go up by 15 per cent. That is because
people are shoved up into higher tax brackets. In the same way, the
corporate, or what you call company, taxation is very much increased
by inflation because depreciation allowances, deductions for inventory,
tend to be based on original costs rather than on market value. As a
result much of what is reported as business profits is a purely paper
profit and not a real profit, and the effect of imposing taxes on those
paper profits is to impose a wealth tax on capital rather than an effective
tax on the returns from capital.

I have made some calculations for the United States of that magnitude.
For the United States that effect alone seems to have amounted to
something like 15 billion dollars in the past year. The return from that
hidden tax was twice as large as the direct return from the straight tax
on cash balances – from the printing of paper money *per se*. I am going
to speak much more from the experience in my own country than
yours. I have talked with numbers of Senators and Representatives, and
everyone of them says the same thing: they never would have legislated
the present level of taxes deliberately and explicitly. They are appalled
at what has happened to the real level of taxes. And yet they have of
course benefited from it and permitted it to occur in an indirect way
through inflation. So I think the indexation of governmental taxes is
essential to improve the political structure, to make legislators face up
to their responsibilities for the taxes they impose as well as for the
expenditures they legislate.

2 The Technicalities of Indexing

In technical detail what is required here is very straightforward and simple in the main. There are some complicated elements to it; I do not want to make it over-simple, but I know in our country, and I am sure this carries over to your country, the essential requirements are, first, that the personal exemptions be expressed in pounds multiplied by a price index. We have a low income allowance – you probably have some similar kind of an allowance – and an automatic deduction or something; whatever it is, it should likewise be expressed in pounds multiplied by an index number. The tax brackets should be expressed not as zero to £1,000, or whatever your surtax brackets are, but as zero to £1,000 multiplied by the price index, so that every year they would be adjusted automatically for inflation. The base for calculating capital gains should be adjusted for the change in price between time of purchase and time of sale. The base for calculating depreciation should be similarly adjusted; so should the base for calculating inventory costs. In principle, you ought to include in profit the gain through the reduction in the real value of obligations expressed in fixed nominal amounts. That ought to be included. There are also some other complications, but the things I have described would eliminate the bulk of the effects of inflation on the real tax rate.

On the side of government borrowing I likewise feel that this is a case of morality and fairness as much as it is of easing the transition. As I have stated several times here, I was myself converted to the issue of government purchasing power securities on a day in 1942 or 1943 when as a very young civil servant in the US Treasury Department I was asked to write a speech for the then Secretary Morganthau to exhort the public to buy US savings bonds. I found it impossible to write an honest speech.

I believe it is absolutely disgraceful that a democracy should demand of its high public officials that they lie to the people they are talking to, and knowingly lie. It is on that ground more than any other that I have ever since that day in 1942 or 1943 been in favour of purchasing power securities being issued by the government.

The argument made against this is the argument Mr Pepper raised again today. It is the argument which the US Treasury Department offered in 1952, when the Joint Economic Committee, as part of a series of hearings on monetary and debt problems, asked academic economists what they thought of purchasing power securities. A very large fraction of academic economists were then in favour of them. The Treasury gave its standard answer, which is exactly the answer in effect that Mr

Pepper is giving today, if I understood him, which was that it would be undesirable to issue purchasing power securities because that would remove an anti-inflationary element from the economy because, they said, if we index – if we have purchasing power securities – inflation will add to our expenditure, whereas at present our expenditures stay the same in nominal dollars, our income is raised, and therefore we have an automatic anti-inflationary force.

3 The Keynesian Theory

That argument is capable of being logically valid but I think it is not empirically relevant. It implicitly assumes that somehow or other the total expenditures of governments are independent of their sources of revenue. A great fallacy in much of the so-called Keynesian analysis has been to suppose that you can treat expenditures as if they were determined by one set of considerations and taxes as if they were determined by another. It is also the great fallacy of people who believe themselves to be in favour of fiscal responsibility – in the United States of many of the Republicans who have preached fiscal responsibility for many years. You have had the peculiar result in the United States over and over again that the Democrats have legislated the expenditures and the Republicans have legislated the taxes to pay for them – under the guise of fiscal responsibility.

Experience by this time has demonstrated Parkinson's law beyond the shadow of a doubt: that legislators will spend whatever the tax system will raise plus a good deal more. And therefore the only effective way to impose fiscal discipline is to reduce tax revenues. Therefore I myself have been converted to the policy of being in favour of tax reductions under any circumstances, for any excuse, for any reason, at any time.

To go back to purchasing power securities, if the government is going to be responsible and stop inflation, it costs nothing to issue a purchasing power security. Indeed the government will gain because they can sell those securities at better terms than they can sell the others. On the other hand, if the government is not going to be responsible, then it does seem to be extremely undesirable, immoral, or whatever other word you want to use, for the government to argue that we cannot issue purchasing power securities because we need this check to keep us responsible. If they are going to be responsible they do not need to worry about any costs imposed by purchasing power securities. And if they are going to be irresponsible, purchasing power securities are needed all the more in order to protect the innocent public from the legislators whom they elected – erroneously.

I'm not sure I have completely answered Mr Pepper's point in that comment and I hope he will come back and pin me down on any further issues in that respect: I interpreted his question to be that if governments are not responsible, will purchasing power bonds make the inflation all the worse because it will increase governmental expenditure? The answer, to repeat it, is: the additional expenditures it will increase are far less harmful to the body politic than the alternative expenditures they will replace.

4 Voluntary Indexation

For the rest, I am not in favour of legislating indexing. I am in favour of encouraging the voluntary adoption of indexing on as wide a scale as possible. And in this position I am in a long and distinguished line. Running back to well before Alfred Marshall, the first evidence of indexing is in Britain in the 14th century when your legislature required the colleges of Oxford and Cambridge to get at least one-third of their rent on their lands in corn, which one-third three centuries later was essentially 100 per cent of their rent. Marshall favoured it, William Stanley Jevons favoured it, Irving Fisher favoured it, John Maynard Keynes favoured it – surprisingly enough.[1] So that I am not here expressing anything of a special view. One of the interesting features I want to call to your attention is that many of the earlier arguments for indexing were as a means of mitigating the undesirable effects of *falling* prices. Marshall, when he wrote in 1885, was writing in a period when you were experiencing a price fall, and in the 1830s or 1820s some of the people who were then advocating indexing were doing so as a way of mitigating the harm being done by the post-Napoleonic war deflation. So that it is not true, as people often say, that those who are proposing indexing are simply proposing that we live with inflation. That is true in a way, but indexing is also a good vehicle for living with deflation.

However, a good money, a responsible money, is a better vehicle than indexing. Indexing is not in and of itself a desirable thing. It is – as I've sometimes said – a second-best device for a first-best world; but it is a first-best device for a second-best world. And the world is unfortunately second-best. At the same time, I see no reason why you should require by law that everybody index – this is what Brazil does – and in their circumstances it has been very effective and the results have been very good. However, I think they have gone much farther than would be desirable for us to go. What we ought to do is to encourage private indexing but not require it.

How do we encourage it? In the first place, the tax changes I have suggested would go a long way to encourage it. If the government offered a purchasing power security, the competition in the private financial market would force private enterprise to issue purchasing power securities as well. Even if the government does not issue a purchasing power security, private enterprises of course are going to offer purchasing power securities. The trend has already started: it is very well advanced in the United States. Empirically speaking, the short-term interest rate has been roughly equal to the rate of rise in prices over the prior several years plus about 3 per cent. And hence the whole series of floating notes, like the Citicorp floating notes in which the rate of return promised is a certain number of points above the Treasury bill rate or a short-term market rate, is economically equivalent to a purchasing power security. That kind of variable interest rate note has already started to spread very widely both in the United States and elsewhere, so you are getting a lot of indexing of that kind.

5   Escalator Clauses

In the wage field in the United States there are something like 10 million union employees covered by cost-of-living escalator clauses. In Britain you did an unwise thing in imposing by legislation a threshold agreement: that was undesirable because it was exactly this imposition of a *general* rule rather than allowing the arrangements to be reached in the *individual* case. But I think that you would and should have a large number of voluntary wage agreements which include an escalator clause.

In many areas now of course there are escalator clauses. You have rental leases which are a fraction of gross; you have automobile insurance policies which pay costs of repairing; all of these have implicit escalator clauses in them. And you are going to have a much wider extension of that kind of escalator clause. The government could encourage it, as I say, first, by setting an example by establishing a kind of instrument through its purchasing power security, second, by the tax changes I have described. Because, under present circumstances, if an enterprise were to offer a purchasing power security, the adjustment for inflation would be subject to income tax as well as the real interest rate paid. The changes I have suggested in the personal and company tax would in effect eliminate that because you would adjust the capital gains basis, and therefore the adjustment for inflation would not be subject to income tax. I think those are the most effective ways in which the government could encourage it.

Now I do not know about your case. In the United States there is one other major area, where I think the government will have to encourage it. This is the so-called thrift institutions.

6 The Financial Intermediaries

We have in the United States, as you have here, savings and loan associations,[2] mutual savings banks, and so on, of very major magnitude. Their total liabilities at the moment are something like $400 billion. These institutions have been 'gambling' for quite a long time by lending long and borrowing short and they are now stuck with a portfolio of lower interest rates than those they now have to pay if they are to keep the funds on deposit with them. If you were to do a proper accounting analysis, there is hardly one of them today that is not *technically* 'bankrupt' in the sense that the market value of its assets is less than the market value of its liabilities.

Being a hard-boiled believer in a free market, I might like to see the market solution work itself out and let a lot of them go broke. But I rather doubt whether that will happen. I rather suspect they will be bailed out by government. I hate like the devil to enter into political prophecy, but this is one of the easiest of any you might make because it has already occurred. There have already been a series of measures to bail them out. But they have been of the wrong kind consistent with the government trying to prop up the value of their capital assets. Along that line you are in a bottomless pit. If you really try to save the savings and loan associations by propping up the market value of their assets, you are going to have to create a quantity of money in the process that is going to blow the lid off the inflation. What is the alternative?

The least bad alternative would be for the government to subsidise thrift institutions on the income side, but subject to the proviso that as a condition of assisting them they must move entirely to an index basis for their assets and liabilities. They must convert to a variable interest rate mortgage which has the effect of being indexed. How you do it is important because some of the ways would not be very effective. You have to do it in a way in which the face value of the mortgage and not merely the repayments are indexed. You have to have a variable interest rate mortgage and you must offer your customers a variable interest deposit. If that were done, the subsidisation programme would automatically end because, as the portfolio turned over and became more and more indexed, you would eliminate the problem that started the process.

Beyond that I would leave it to the voluntary interests of people to engage in indexing and not try to enforce it in any way. The question comes up: what good does it do to have all these things indexed? The major objection I have heard arises out of a misconception. The objection I have heard here today and in Britain several times in the past few days is that somehow or other indexing would prevent real wages from being reduced where it is economically necessary for them to be reduced. Indexing prevents no such thing. Indexing is a provision to adjust contractual terms between re-contracting. When a new contract is negotiated, it can be at a higher or a lower or any real wage whatsoever. All that indexing does is to say: whatever two people agree on, they will in fact achieve. It is only a way of enabling people to engage in effective contracts. Today, if a contract is made between an employer and, let us say, a trade union or a non-union group, both of them have to make a guess about the rate of inflation. If they agree on the rate of inflation, they will build. it into contracted increase.

If the actual rate of inflation is equal to the anticipated rate, nobody is disappointed and there is no distortion. But if the actual rate of inflation is different from the expected rate, one or the other party has engaged in a contract he did not voluntarily engage in: he's got distorted terms. It is this feature that is largely responsible for the unemployment which results from a slowing down of the rate of inflation that is *not* anticipated and that has not been built into these contracts. By indexing you eliminate that disappointment and distortion. Parties can contract to whatever terms they want. They can contract in real terms.

I said earlier that I thought it cleared the mind analytically to try to carry out an analysis in a world of complete indexing. But it not only clears the mind; it also in practice would prevent some of the adverse effects from slowing down inflation, or some of the adverse effects from an acceleration of inflation. It is on those grounds that I think indexing would be extremely useful and I think it is in that area that the experience of Brazil is most important.

7 Indexing and Authoritarianism

I hesitate to refer to Brazil because I have been burned so badly. The moment I refer to Brazil I am told: Oh, you like a military dictatorship? No, I do not: military dictatorships are terrible. But I think as scientists we ought to pick up our data wherever we can get them, from communist Russia, from Nazi Germany, from totalitarian Brazil, from wherever we can get good economic evidence. We do not have enough data so that we can afford to let our scientific analyses be determined by our political sympathies.

And the evidence from Brazil and from other countries is very striking. It is that you can greatly reduce distortion by a widespread use of indexing.

DISCUSSION

GEORGE SCHWARTZ: With the 'greenback' debacle in the middle of the 19th century private people did index their contracts by inserting a gold clause. What happened to that solemn contract between private people agreeing that the terms of the contract should be based on the gold clause? It was arbitrarily abrogated by the Roosevelt administration. Are you in the US going to write a guarantee into your constitution? – We can't because we haven't got a constitution! What guarantee is there with any of these methods? In my lifetime government has proved to be a liar, a thief, and a cheat. And I don't see any difference today.

FRIEDMAN: I have no answer to the fundamental question of guarantees but I do think it is important to understand the gold clause a little better. It is rather more complicated than George Schwartz's intervention might suggest.

I agree with him that the Supreme Court should not have abrogated it. But it is interesting to read the relevant decisions of the Supreme Court. In large part they rested on the fact that while the gold clause was entered into to protect people in real value, enforcement of the gold clause would not achieve that purpose. The argument which induced a majority of the Supreme Court justices to abrogate the gold clause was that in 1933, when the issue arose, although the gold price had risen in nominal terms, the level of prices of goods and services in general had fallen, and so the majority on the Supreme Court said that people who were being paid back in dollars were already making one gain from the decline of the price level. It was not in the interests of equity and justice that they should make a second gain because the dollar price of gold was being raised by the authorities.

It turns out on reading those decisions that had those clauses been purchasing power clauses it is very far from clear that the US Supreme Court would have abrogated them. This is a footnote to history and does not alter your main point that I have no more assurance that a privately arranged escalator contract will be enforced in the Courts than I have that any other private contract will be enforced in the Courts. I don't see anything special about it. On your grounds you would suppose that nobody would enter into any contract because there is no contract that you can be sure will be enforced.

NICHOLAS RIDLEY:[3]   I would like to go back to the question of the indexed government securities Professor Friedman talked about. When I approached the British Treasury Ministers asking why they did not introduce an indexed government security, they said that it would do too much harm to the values of the existing government debt. We have a nominal of about £30,000 million worth of government debt, which is currently valued in the markets at about £14,000 million, having gone down £5,000 million in the last year. If it dropped another £10,000 million due to the issue of an indexed bond this would obviously be very serious politically to the poor mugs who still hold war loan. Would Professor Friedman comment on that argument? Would the higher interest rate check too much selling and bring in buyers as it started to rise? Does he believe there would be serious disruptive effects upon existing holders of government stock if fully indexed bonds were issued?

FRIEDMAN: That is a very good, a very fundamental, question. Let us take it up a little bit at a time, because it is necessary to proceed piecemeal.

The question is at what rate the indexed bonds are going to be issued. One way would be to auction them off. That might lead to a negative real rate being set by the market. If you conceive of governments issuing their indexed bonds by auctioning them off, but with the index clause inserted, there is no reason why that should produce any serious disruption whatsoever to the value of outstanding securities. Gradually as time went on, as more and more indexed bonds were sold in the market, the real rate offered would have to go up. But if without indexing inflation accelerates, the value of these bonds is going to fall anyway. If inflation decelerates, it will go the opposite way. If indeed the issuance of indexed bonds is accompanied by a responsible monetary policy which produces a deceleration of inflation, you will suffer no loss in the market value of the other bonds. On the contrary, they will rise. If it is accompanied by an irresponsible policy, you will indeed suffer a loss on the other bonds, as you would anyway. So I really do not think that, once you look at it in that realistic way of issuing these bonds on an auction basis, you will necessarily get into any kind of problem at all.

LORD ROBBINS: You have to remember that opinion in Whitehall to some extent is governed, although perhaps now unconsciously, by a dictum of the late Arthur Balfour who was one of the few intellectuals who have been Prime Minister of this country: he said that no government is prepared to legislate on the assumption of its own irresponsibility.

FRIEDMAN: I agree, and I do not want them to do that. I want them to legislate on the assumption of their *responsibility*, because that means it costs them nothing if they are really responsible. It not only costs them nothing to issue indexed bonds – they gain, because they can issue them at a *negative* interest rate to begin with.

GORDON PEPPER: Having been invited to make a rejoinder – I have no argument at all about the morals. I am assuming that we have a government that does immoral things, and which is capable of expanding the money supply in the same way as in 1972–3. If I heard correctly, you argued that index-linking helps even if inflation is accelerating. I did not fully follow and I do not fully understand.

I am afraid that what happened after the introduction of floating exchange rates may happen with index-linking. After floating exchange rates were introduced, the government followed a completely irresponsible monetary policy – the resulting downward movement in sterling accelerated inflation. We have only a limited period of time before the height of inflation in this country undermines our democratic structure. During that period we must try to educate MPs, people in Whitehall and people in power. I do not want to see the government misusing index-linking – making mistakes similar to 1972–3 and causing inflation to accelerate that much faster. We may have only one more cycle rather than another two or three cycles. The other point which I tried to make earlier concerns indexing of wages. If, because of practical reasons of one form or another, it is impossible to index wages, is not some form of wages policy a second-best method of trying to bias the outcome of a reduction in the rate of growth of the money supply towards a greater reduction in price inflation and a smaller reduction in real economic activity?

FRIEDMAN: Those are very good questions. With respect, I would like to enter a demur about the floating exchange rate aspect. I think it was irresponsible government policy that made it necessary to devalue. It was a continuation of irresponsible government policy that caused further depreciation. I think it is irresponsible government policy today in your country that is keeping the exchange rate up. From the long-run point of view – if I understand your situation properly – it just seems to me insane for your government to be giving exchange guarantees on any large amount of sterling whether to oil countries or anybody else. As I understand it, they have been doing that. Is that right? So I do not believe you can blame the floating exchange rates for the irresponsible policies, but quite the other way around.

On your direct question: let us answer the question, how is it that index-linking of bonds would accelerate inflation? Mr Pepper would undoubtedly reply that, if you index-link the bonds, then as time passes, as inflation accelerates, your necessary governmental expenditures are increased. That is true. The question is *how* you index-link bonds. You can index-link bonds in two very different ways. One way is by saying that the maturity value or face value will at the time of redemption be multiplied by an index number, and the annual coupon will be multiplied by an index number, so that a bond that would otherwise pay a £3 per £100 yield would pay £3.30 if inflation were 10 per cent. But the face value instead of being £100 would now be raised to £110.

The other way is to pay each year the face coupon rate plus the rate

of inflation. So the face value would remain £100, and you would pay
£3 plus £10, that is 13 per cent. Now it may look as if this second way
gets you into the dilemma you're speaking of, whereas the first does
not. But that is wrong, they are both equivalent. The second way
essentially involves your paying off the debt, you are amortising the
debt, that 10 per cent payment means that you are reducing the real
burden of the debt and therefore you can afford to borrow more, as
it were, at the same interest rate. So that the effect of indexing is not
to add to your annual interest payment requirements the rate of
inflation times the debt, but only the rate of inflation times the interest
payments. In terms of magnitude I am suggesting to you that what
you are talking about is much smaller than you might otherwise
suppose.

Now offsetting this effect, which no doubt is there in that indexing
would tend to increase expenditure on interest payments, is that it
would tend to reduce other expenditures. If we go back to the principle
I was citing earlier, which I think is true: that what is really given to
you more or less is the deficit which a government is willing to run,
so that total expenditures are determined by adding to that deficit
whatever the tax system will yield – the major effect in my opinion of
indexing would be that the heavier pressure of interest payments to
meet the indexed security rates would impose on you the necessity of
cutting other expenditure.

Finally, suppose you do not index. Then you have a situation in
which it is extremely hard to sell long-dated securities. I am sure that
as a stockbroker you do not have as good a market for long-dated
securities now as you had in the period when prices were stable. But
if you sell short-dated securities, the market imposes the effect of
indexing on the Treasury because you can sell short-dated securities
only at a price which allows for the anticipated inflation. For a long
time you have been able to con the purchasers into believing that the
rate of inflation was going to be less than it was. But doesn't that
come to an end? And may it not indeed be that the effect of not
indexing will be to make the annual expenditures of the government
on interest higher than with indexed bonds, because expectations will
run ahead of the reality and force up the interest rates the government
has to pay, even higher than would be enough to justify it. All I am
trying to argue is that there are forces running in different directions.

8 Incomes 'Policies': the Case of Argentina

Now let me go to your other question about wages policy. I want to associate myself with one of the comments of David Laidler. (I hope it's safe to say at this time and in this place and in this country that he got some of his training at the University of Chicago.) I want to associate myself very much with his comment about not using the phrase 'wage policies or incomes policies' if what you mean is governmental *control* of wages and prices. We in the United States have got very badly hurt by that misuse of terminology. And you also are likely to. People say to me that by 'incomes policy' all they mean is improving the markets and letting the free markets operate. I am for those kinds of incomes policies. But what you are really talking about is whether the fixing of wages and prices could enable you to achieve an easier transition. I cannot rule out the possibility completely, because I know of one empirical case in which it did work – the case of Argentina. One year back in the 1960s a government was determined to end an inflation – a rare event in Argentina! It was very substantial, not your moderate kind of inflation. It was about 40–50 per cent. They announced a new monetary policy which was going to be very strict and they accompanied it by a temporary fixing of prices and wages. By altering people's expectations, and cutting off the tendency for wages to rise in line with anticipated inflation, they did succeed in rather substantially reducing the rate of inflation with relatively little cost in the way of unemployment. Needless to say, this was a temporary success. It was followed by another blow-up a few years later. So it is hardly a permanent answer.

I cannot rule out the theoretical possibility that a measure like that might be to some extent successful. But that is a very exceptional case. It was possible only because you were dealing with rates of inflation of 40 or 50 per cent. When you deal with what are really relatively low rates of inflation you are not proposing this wage and price freeze or control for more than six months. Let us leave out all political considerations for a moment; let us suppose you can do it for a six-month period. Then what are you doing?

Let us suppose you are faced with a 20 per cent inflation. You are trying to change people's expectations from a 10 per cent rise in prices over that period to, say a zero per cent rise in prices. In the process you are preventing changes in *relative* prices and wages, many of which will be multiples of 10 per cent. So you are introducing a whole series of *distortions* of a very considerable kind into your price structure. You can have exactly the same result far better if, without any wage policy, the people can be made to believe that the government is serious in its anti-inflation effort. In reality your wage proposal will not work unless people believe the government is serious.

The next stage of getting away from this purely hypothetical case of the best of all circumstances is the reality that wage and price controls will be adopted only as a means of enabling the government to inflate more than it otherwise would. Those of you who argue for wage and price policy on this kind of a valid argument are in fact lending support to an inflationary policy, because the empirical evidence is that every government imposes wage and price controls when it intends to inflate.

It does so because it wants to give the public the impression that it is doing something about inflation when it really does not want to do something. That describes Mr Heath's freeze here. It describes Mr Nixon's freeze in August 1971. Let me supplement David Laidler's historical account of the British experience with an account of the American experience, which is equally informative.

9 American Experience

In 1969–70 we adopted a restraining monetary policy. It worked like a charm. The rate of price inflation fell from roughly 7 per cent sometime in 1969 to something like $4\frac{1}{2}$ per cent at the time of the freeze on 15 August 1971. So in about 15 or 16 months we had come down from something like 7 per cent (which had been accelerating, so that the real comparison is between where it *would* have gone to with *continuation* of prior inflation) to 4 per cent with the mildest recession in the post-war period.

In 1970–71 the economy had already turned up: we were expanding. The rate of inflation was still coming down. But two events occurred. One was that the consequences of our mistaken gold policy were finally coming home to roost, and something had to be done to close the gold window. The other was that there was still a lagged reaction to earlier experience which was leading politicians of all parties to yell and scream about how terrible the recession was: we were not moving fast enough and had to move faster. All of this was combined with Mr Nixon's great concern for a favourable economic climate for the 1972 election. The combination of these events led him on 15 August 1971 to close the gold window – which by itself would have been very unpopular – and to cover it up with the price and wage freeze and with an announcement of measures intended to stimulate employment. There is no doubt that the price and wage freeze were undertaken in order to permit an inflationary policy to follow thereafter.

I believe our present situation dates precisely from that date; the origin of our troubles is there. As David Laidler said, the initial effects of an inflationary policy were on output, its subsequent effects on prices, though they were hidden for a time by the price and wage controls. The controls finally blew up and had to be abandoned. Our present recorded 12 per cent rate of inflation is a statistical fake. The true rate of inflation is not 12 per cent. Part of it is the unveiling of price increases that were suppressed during the price control period, and part of it is that every businessman who has any sense, which includes every businessman, is trying to get his base prices up as high as he can in case there is another price and wage freeze. And that is why the actual experience in the United States is that we are going to see a very sharp tapering off in the recorded rates of inflation.

This process is going to come to an end, the truth is going to be told, and you are going to have a recorded decline in the rate of inflation. The danger there is the one David Laidler mentioned, that everyone will breathe a sigh of relief and say – My God, isn't this wonderful! We're back at only 8 per cent inflation! – Only 8 per cent! – when it was $4\frac{1}{2}$ per cent when Nixon imposed price and wage control. And they are going to say: we have got to do something about unemployment . . . .

Notes

1   Cf. Brian Griffiths, 'English Classical Political Economy and the Debate on Indexation', in *Monetary Correction*, Occasional Paper 41, IEA, 1974.
2   [The British equivalent is the building societies. The fundamental difference is that the US institutions lend with fixed interest rates, whereas building society mortgages have variable interest rates. Building societies also issue variable rate investments. – ED.]
3   Parliamentary Under-Secretary of State, Department of Trade and Industry, 1970–72.

7

From Galbraith to Economic Freedom

I The Conventional Wisdom of J. K. Galbraith

1 Introduction

I want to start out by explaining that I have no prejudice against John Kenneth Galbraith. Indeed some of my best friends are Galbraithians, including John Kenneth. I say this because there is often somewhat of a tendency to attribute to motives what is really to be attributed to honest difference of opinion. Galbraith deserves a good deal of credit for his independence of mind, for his diligence in trying to spread and promote his ideas, and for an attempt to put intellectual content into some of them.

I mean that seriously. For example, in one policy which is rather peripheral to his general body of thought, namely that of price and wage control, Kenneth Galbraith has the company of many other people from many other points of view who are in favour of, or have from time to time espoused, wage and price control, but so far as I know, he is the only person who has made a serious attempt to present a theoretical analysis to justify his position, in a book called *A Theory of Price Control*[1] he wrote not long after World War II. I happen to think that the analysis is wrong, but at least it is a serious attempt to provide a basis for a point of view.

There are even some subjects and some issues on which he and I have been in agreement. The most important of those, I think, in the United

This chapter comprises the substance of two talks delivered to IEA audiences on 31 August and 1 September 1976; published originally as IEA Occasional Paper No. 49 (1977).

States setting, was the question of military conscription. Kenneth Galbraith, like me, was for many years a strong and public opponent of military conscription, and this despite that some of his closest political allies – for example, Senator Edward Kennedy – were on the other side of the argument. Also, not quite two years ago, when shortly after he became President, Mr Ford assembled a summit meeting of various groups of people to advise him on inflation, I was fascinated to find that at a meeting of economists Galbraith was one of the few outside of those whom you would expect to take this position – the so-called 'liberal' economists – to take the problem of inflation seriously and to regard it as something which had to be corrected.

2 Conviction and Documentation

Having said this, I want to proceed to analyse his thought and his position, but I do so, as I say, with full respect for him as an individual and for his independence. The puzzle I find on reading Galbraith, and the one which will provide something of a theme for what I have to say, is how to reconcile his own sincere *conviction* in the validity of his view of the world with the almost complete failure of any other students – even those who are sympathetic with his general political orientation – to *document* its validity. There have been many people who have looked at his picture of the world, but, although there must be some exceptions, I do not know of any serious scholars who have validated his conception. Kenneth Galbraith has obviously read these criticisms and seen these arguments. The puzzle I want to propose for you is how to reconcile his conviction in the validity of that view with the failure of others to document it.

Affluence for whom?

The typical conventional approach to the conventional wisdom of John Kenneth Galbraith has been to treat him as if he were trying to examine and describe the world and then to compare the position he arrives at with reality. In briefly surveying this conventional approach we may start with *The Affluent Society*,[2] a book, interestingly enough, which was published just before the 'war on poverty' became a widespread obsession. Now I may say I regard that as less of a reflection on Galbraith than on the proponents of the war on poverty. In the fundamental point of view that we are indeed a relatively affluent society, Galbraith was entirely correct. The war on poverty of which so much has been made since then has been a very good thing indeed for many thousands of civil servants who have been able to make excellent careers and many thousands of academic people who have been able to do study after study on poverty. But it has not done very much to help the people who are most disadvantaged in our economy and society.

The main content of the book was not really the affluence of society. Rather it was devoted to other themes: to denigrating the tastes of ordinary people, the tastes of those who prefer pushpin to poetry, who prefer large tailfins to nice, compact, expensive little cars. It was directed to developing the advantages of extending the power of government. A major theme was the alleged contrast between private affluence and public squalor.

In mentioning the criticisms which were made of that theme I must make a start with a review of Galbraith's 1958 *Affluent Society* written by Adam Smith in 1776. I quote from Adam Smith:

> It is the highest impertinence and presumption in kings and ministers to pretend to watch over the economy of private people and to restrain their expense either by sumptuary laws or by prohibiting the importation of foreign luxuries. They are themselves always and without any exception the greatest spendthrifts in the society. Let them look well after their own expenses and they may safely trust private people with theirs. If their own extravagance does not ruin the state, that of their subjects never will.

So I think most of us would agree that 'public affluence and private penury' comes closer to a correct description of the world. I cannot resist adding another of Smith's devastating comments, not so immediately relevant to Galbraith's book but it is a little.

> There is no art which one government sooner learns of another than that of draining money from the pockets of the people.

That is an art which certainly your government and my government have learned very well.

The general reaction of his contemporaries was not much different from Adam Smith's reaction. There was widespread criticism of Galbraith's denigration of public attitudes in terms of his being a 'tailfin burner', like the book burner of an earlier day. Who was he to tell people what they should like?

Galbraith and advertising

There was an examination of his animadversions on advertising. You will recall that one of the main themes in *The Affluent Society* was the enormous power which Galbraith assigned to advertising: that these tastes for tailfins were not natural or native, that they were created by greedy producers seeking to shape the tastes of the public to satisfy their own interests. There resulted a considerable expansion in the economic analysis of advertising which tended to demonstrate, first, that a very large fraction of all advertising was informative rather than persuasive, secondly, that even in persuasive advertising the smart and intelligent thing for an enterprise to do was to find out what the public wants and then make it and advise them of it, not to try to shape its tastes. But, more important from Galbraith's general point of view, there was a great deal of emphasis on the extent to which you had advertising not only by private enterprise but also by government and bureaucrats, and that this has at least as widespread an effect as private advertising.

The statistics on government spending made Galbraith's theme of private affluence versus public squalor an absurd claim. Anybody who studies the statistics knows that government spending has grown apace. In the United States it has grown from about 10 per cent of the national income in 1929 to something over 40 per cent today. In the United Kingdom it has grown from 10 per cent of the national income at the time of the Diamond Jubilee of Queen Victoria to something like 60 per cent today. It is very hard, in the face of these figures, to maintain the claim that it is the private spendthrifts and not the public spendthrifts who are impoverishing the nation.

Countervailing power – the 'unholy trinity'?

Let me go on from his affluent society to his theory of countervailing power,[3] a book to which George Stigler once addressed a devastating review under the title 'The Economist Plays with Blocs'.[4] The thesis which Galbraith set up in that book was that when concentrations of power arise they stimulate countervailing concentrations of power. Big business stimulates big labour, and both stimulate big government. And the combination of big business, big labour, and big government is a holy, not an unholy, trinity.

The answer to this thesis given by George Stigler and by other critics has been that it is a mistake to suppose that these concentrated groups are always on *different* sides. After all, big business and big labour have *common* interests *vis-à-vis* the consumer. It will be in the self-interest of both groups to operate together to exploit the consumer. In any event, far from this being a countervailing power, or a power that would restore stability and offset the harm done by large conglomerations, it intensifies the harm. Cartel agreements are unstable; and agreements among bilateral or multilateral monopolists are unstable. In any case, the whole Galbraithian argument is factually incorrect. The evidence is that some of the *largest* concentrations of union power are in industries in which the employers have very *little* concentration of power. In the United States, for example, the coal miners' is a major concentrated union, able to gain advantages for its members by acting as a monopolising agent for the industry because the industry itself is so *dispersed*. The coal miners in effect run a cartel on behalf of the employers. Similarly, the teamsters' union, certainly one of the strongest in the United States, did not arise as a countervailing power to some pre-existing corporate monopoly. It arose in part because there was *dispersed* power from which it was able to benefit.

Whither the 'new industrial state'?

This theme of countervailing power is one to which Kenneth Galbraith has in recent years paid almost no attention. He has largely dropped it by the wayside because he has discovered a more attractive way to approach the same objective. And that is through his most ambitious book, *The New Industrial State*,[5] in which he seeks to bring up to date Thorstein Veblen's *The Engineers and the Price System* 'with a good deal of help from James Burnham's *The Managerial Revolution*.[7]

This book implied largely a rejection of the thesis of countervailing power in favour of the thesis that control of society is in the hands of a technical–managerial class, the 'technostructure'. One of Galbraith's great abilities is his ability to seize upon key words and sell them. He is an advertiser *par excellence!* It has always puzzled me why the commercial advertising industry has not recognised that and taken advantage of his extraordinary quality. 'The affluent society' was one such phrase. 'Countervailing power' was another. Now somehow I would think that if you started out with such a clumsy word as 'technostructure' it would not exactly become a common saying, a household word – yet it seems to have caught on very well indeed! The key theme of *The New Industrial State*, as you all know, is that the economy is dominated by giant concerns in which control is in the hands of the technical–managerial class. These have grown so large that individuals are no longer important as entrepreneurs: stockholders play a purely passive role of approving whatever actions management takes and serve no important entre-preneurial function.

This managerial class, according to Galbraith, has as its chief aim security for itself. And it seems to achieve that security by controlling both those who supply goods and services to the enterprise and those who purchase its product. It seems to control both suppliers and deman-ders, and it does so, of course, with the aid of government. It establishes an effective coalition with the governmental authorities. And together with government it can secure its own future.

It controls its suppliers by being a monopolistic purchaser, the prime source of demand for their products. It controls the demanders by the use of persuasive advertising. This theme from *The Affluent Society* is one that is central to Galbraith's view throughout this whole series of books. In his view the market plays a very minor rôle indeed. True, there remain some enterprises such as agriculture, small service trades, and so on, which are essentially competitive enterprises subject to market control and market pressure. But they are a tail that is wagged by the dog of the large corporate giants, which in Galbraith's view typify the modern economy.

This view has also been examined and attacked by many scholars. John Jewkes, in his book on *The Sources of Invention*,[8] examines Gal-braith's claim that the day of the small enterpriser is past, that, in Galbraith's words as quoted by Jewkes, 'a benign providence has made the modern industry of a few large firms an almost perfect instrument for inducing technical change'. Jewkes examines this claim and writes at the close of his book:

> Nearly all the systematic evidence has run counter to any such doctrine. Yet, so far as we are aware, Professor Galbraith has said nothing in defence, or in modification, of his views.[9]

Lack of realism and understanding

The validity of Galbraith's picture of the industrial world was attacked from a very different point of view by Sir Frank McFadzean, who is sitting here in the audience and so can correct me if I misrepresent his critique. Sir Frank attacked Galbraith for a lack of realism, and misunderstanding of how large enterprises are run. He attacked the realism of Galbraith's view from the inside, as it were, and demonstrated, I think rather conclusively in a lecture he gave some 10 years ago,[10] that the notion that somehow or other large enterprises were run by faceless impersonal committees with the ability to control their future was a fairy-tale rather than an accurate description.

Galbraith was similarly attacked by Professor G. C. Allen in an excellent *Paper*[11] published by the Institute of Economic Affairs, on similar grounds, but with rather more attention to the behaviour of aggregates, such as industry as a whole, than to the behaviour of particular enterprises. Finally, some studies have been made by an American economist, Harold Demsetz, formerly at the University of Chicago but currently at the University of California at Los Angeles; he tested three of the Galbraithian hypotheses statistically to see whether the facts coincided with them. Galbraith had emphasised that defence industries were the examples *par excellence* of industries that were capable of controlling their own destinies because they had the government for a client and could effectively control the demand for their products, the prices at which they sold, and the like. Demsetz proceeded to examine the evidence.[12] He examined the market behaviour of the stocks of 13 large defence-oriented industries in the United States. Lo and behold, he found that the real return from investing in those stocks was much more variable from year to year than the average of all other stocks! It may have been necessary at that time to go to the stock market, but one need merely today observe the fate of some of the defence giants in the United States like Lockheed, General Dynamic and the like, to recognise that they are very, very far indeed from being in a position to control their own destiny. And not even very large expenditures on persuasive advertising in foreign countries enables them to do so.

'No evidence'

Professor Demsets also examined two other hypotheses of Galbraith's. You would find his article[13] extremely interesting because he points out how difficult it is to get testable hypotheses out of the Galbraithian canon. Galbraith speaks in broad general terms; he makes assertions about the world at large. But they are very seldom put in a form in which they yield testable hypotheses. In addition to the one about defence industries, Demsetz tested, through multiple correlation of the experience of many enterprises, the Galbraithian theme that technostructure-oriented firms sacrifice profits to accelerate the growth of sales. Galbraith's theme here is that once you get one of these large corporations with the technocrats in the technostructure in command, they have to have certain minimal profits in order to satisfy the stockholders and keep them quiet, but beyond that what they really want to do is to grow. And so, argues Galbraith, they are willing to sacrifice profits for the sake of sales. Demsetz proceeded to assemble data on firms and to classify them as technostructure-oriented by the kind of criteria Galbraith used. He then tried to see whether it was true that there was a trade-off of profits against sales. *He could find no evidence for it whatsoever.*

He also investigated Galbraith's thesis that such firms use the control of prices, of advertising and of government intervention to prevent the disruption of their plans. Again he did this by trying to see whether firms of that type in practice have more stable income and profits than other firms. Again he found no confirmation at all of this Galbraithian claim.

Misinterpretation of economic theory and research

There have been many other criticisms of Galbraith's views, including many by people who are politically very sympathetic to his orientation, such as for example the extremely critical review of *The New Industrial State* by Robert Solow,[14] in which he criticised Galbraith as misinterpreting both economic theory and recent research. The claim that the managers can neglect the stockholders because enterprises are large has itself been subjected to an enormous amount of study. We all know that the stock market exerts an influence in a very indirect but effective way. And, no matter how large the enterprise, if the managers act in such a way as to earn less than is feasible with those resources, this has an effect on the price of the stock. If the stock price is driven down it provides somebody with an incentive to buy up the stock, engage in take-over activity, and in this way kick out the current management. And there have been enough cases of this occurring for every manager in every major enterprise to recognise where his own self-interest lies.

It is very interesting indeed that the enterprises which come closest, in my opinion, to conforming to Galbraith's picture of the modern giants are some of the *nationalised* industries, because there indeed there is no effective stock market to enforce on the managers the promotion of the interests of the enterprise.

The main purpose of going over this examination of the evidence is that, so far as I know, apart from Galbraith's own assertion, *there has been no successful defence of this view of the world.* That does not mean there are no defenders of the view. There are many. There are many who accept it. But I know of no scientific studies which have validated that view of the world as meaningful and accurate in the sense that it yields predictions about the behaviour of enterprises, of industry, or of the economy as a whole that can be checked, tested against evidence, and found to hold.

3 Galbraith – Scientist or Missionary?

And that brings me back to the puzzle I started with. How can so intelligent, thoughtful and independent a mind as Kenneth Galbraith's hold such an apparently indefensible view of reality? The basis for an answer, I think, is to be found by re-examining Galbraith's purpose and approach. Instead of regarding him as a scientist seeking explanations, I think we shall get more understanding if we look at him as a missionary seeking converts. We must therefore examine not his evidence, not his hypotheses, but his values and his philosophy, his ideology. If we do so I think we shall see that his view of the world derives from his ideological view, and not the other way round.

Galbraith a Tory Radical?

Galbraith has always seemed to me a 20th-century version of the early 19th-century Tory Radicals of Great Britain. Some of you will have read a book by Cecil Driver called *Tory Radical: The Life of Richard Oastler*.[15] At any rate, there was a group of Tories in the early 19th century called Tory Radicals, whose position was, as I see it, very similar to Galbraith's position today. They believed in an aristocracy, as he does. They knew they were members of that aristocracy, as he does. They had membership in it by virtue of birth; he has membership in it by virtue of other qualities. They believed that the aristocracy had an obligation to the masses and that they were the only disinterested group in the community that could serve the masses, because their position came to them naturally, without effort necessarily on their part, and this provided them with an obligation at the same time that it in large measure assured their disinterestedness. They believed, however, that they should not – and Galbraith believes that he should not – use force to impose their views on the masses. Their approach was fully paternalistic: they were in a position of a father to children, whose children would naturally recognise the superiority of the father and that his values were superior to theirs. And so the Tory Radicals expected, and thought it appropriate, that the masses would accept the dominion of the aristocrats over their values and beliefs, because the aristocrats were seeking their welfare. I believe that Galbraith's view is essentially the same. He is not in favour of any kind of imposition on the masses of the values he stands for. He knows that his values are superior to those of the masses, and he thinks that if the masses are properly instructed by enough of his books, they will come themselves to that view and will ask him and his fellow intellectuals to take charge.

He has thus always reminded me of the Tory Radicals, but Shirley and William Letwin[16] and others have persuaded me that there is also a strong admixture of John Stuart Mill's philosophical radicalism. I can demonstrate that element most quickly and effectively by reading a few quotations from Maurice Cowling's book on *Mill and Liberalism.*[17] You will see that each of these quotations, which Maurice Cowling regards as applicable to John Stuart Mill, is every bit as applicable to Galbraith.

First:

> ... 'the higher minds' should set the tone of the society in which they live; and hence ... *their* sort of education in general culture must be propagated as extensively as possible. (p. 37)

Second:

> ... Mill's fundamental principles have neither proof nor philosophical authority, but are commitments to action, the outcome of assertions to claim knowledge of the nature of the world and the direction men's duty ought to take within it: ... it is difficult to avoid feeling that much of what we will characterise as his *arrogance* is connected with want of clarity at this point. (p. 77)

Note that 'want of clarity' is about whether his assertions have scientific authority.

There is no-one who does not apply the word 'arrogant' to Galbraith, and with justice. It applies precisely for the reason that Cowling refers to it in Mill: because Galbraith treats his assertions as if they have scientific authority, as if they have been demonstrated, when they have not been at all. His principles, as Cowling says about Mill's, are commitments to action.

Third:

> Mill was one of the most censorious of 19th-century moralists. At every turn, denigration of existing society is offered with inquisitorial certainty .... (p. 143)

Finally:

> If a writer believes a doctrine he is promulgating, and feels an obligation to it, he is unlikely to reveal its limitations. (p. 147)

Reconciling lack of evidence with dogmatic conviction

That brings me back to my main theme: the reconciliation of the factual inadequacy of the Galbraithian view and the dogmatic confidence with which he asserts it. I want to show how you can link the position he takes about the world with his ideological and philosophical view.

First, Galbraith's Tory Radical position implies that the values of the masses are inferior to those of the intellectual aristocracy, and that, of course, is the theme that runs throughout his analysis. But, moreover, if the values of the masses are created by self-interested advocates in industry, then they have no claim to be considered as valid, or to be respected. Thus, in order for Galbraith to strengthen his emphasis on the right of the aristocracy to shape the values of the masses, it is extremely convenient to be able to treat those values as having no validity but simply as the creation of self-interested advocates.

This has further implications. If it is possible for values to be altered by advertising, Mill's 'higher minds' can affect them too. After all, if these commercial advertisers can shape man's life, there is meaning to having a society in which the higher minds can shape man's wants and values. And you can have some success from this Tory radical political programme of the leading aristocrats, so there is point to having them in power.

Moreover, if you have rule by a free market, if a free market really ruled in response to valid consumer wants, that would provide an alternative to rule by higher minds. It would also render such rule difficult or impossible to achieve. Many reformers – Galbraith is not alone in this – have as their basic objection to a free market that it frustrates them in achieving their reforms, because it enables people to have what they want, not what the reformers want. Hence every reformer has a strong tendency to be adverse to a free market. Galbraith in particular must regard it as trivial or non-existent, or else his whole ideological case, both its justification and its possibility, collapses.

If the free market is not the ruler, who are the rulers? Not, according to Galbraith, entrepreneurs serving the market, but technocrats, who have no moral authority. Besides, they are not disinterested. These technocrats are self-selected, they make their own jobs, they appoint one another. What right do they have to decide people's tastes, or how the resources of a community should be used? If you had Adam Smith entrepreneurs running the society in response to the demands of the public, that would have some moral authority. But the technocrats have no moral authority: they are running it in their own interest.

I believe that this is a very important feature in the Galbraithian view. It serves both to justify his emphasis on rule by the intellectual class and also to enhance its appeal to the public at large. We all want somebody to blame things on. Nothing that happens that is bad is our fault; it's other people who do it to us. And all the better if those other people are faceless bureaucrats in the private sector whom we did not elect, we did not choose. They just somehow got there.

Incidentally, if the technocracy rules, if the technocracy fixes prices and wages for its own convenience, then government officials can do so also. However, as I mentioned earlier, Galbraith's attitude towards price and wage control is not really central to his position. You can subtract it and leave his position unaltered. It is really peripheral to it; it arises out of the sheer accident that he happened to spend part of World War II as a price controller.

This interpretation of Galbraith's view of the world seems to me to make it all of one piece and explains his stubbornness in adhering to it. The characteristics he attributes to the world are essential to upholding his values, his ideological and his political position. But it also explains the grounds on which other people object to it, including myself. The philosophical radicals, like the socialists, attacked the aristocracy. In this they were quite a bit different from Galbraith. On the other hand, they were similar to Galbraith in that insofar as there were to be leaders they wanted them to be a meritocracy rather than an aristocracy. And in this respect Galbraith joins them.

Meritocracy or aristocracy – the lesser evil

I must say I object to being ruled either by the natural-born aristocracy or by a meritocracy but, if I have to be ruled by either, it seems to me that aristocracy of birth is much the lesser evil if only because those who are born to be aristocrats are less likely to be arrogant. They know it is an accident. This was of course the endearing feature of the Tory Radicals, that they recognised they were accidentally in the position of leadership. This is what, in their view, gave them their obligations to the rest of the community, their *noblesse oblige*. But a meritocracy, people who know that they are *abler* than their fellows, and are therefore in a position to rule? Heaven forbid!

More fundamentally, of course, I object to the view that *any* aristocracy should rule. I believe it is of the utmost arrogance for any of us to suppose that we have the right to decide what is the better and the worse value for others by any means other than persuasion. We may of course have strong views of our own: we may believe very strongly that poetry is better than pushpin, or the reverse. But for those of us who believe in the dignity of the individual human being, in the pre-eminence of freedom among human beings as the objective of social organisation: we must say that the only way in which we have any right to try to affect the values of others is by persuasion. And that, I may say, includes commercial advertising, which I view as a form of free speech and which ought to be just as much subject as other forms of discourse to the First Amendment of the United States Constitution prohibiting governmental measures against free speech. (The US Supreme Court, I am delighted to say, has recently so ruled.)

Galbraith versus Adam Smith

These are, I believe, the fundamental grounds on which the battle is drawn. Throughout all history there have been the superiors who have believed that they have the right to rule the inferiors. And the only method of social and economic organisation that has ever been developed which avoids that result is the method which Adam Smith espoused in his *Wealth of Nations*: voluntary co-operation among individuals in which each man is free to use his own capacities and resources as he wills in accordance with his own values so long as he does not interfere with the right of others to do likewise. That is a view of the world which is profoundly opposed by the Galbraithian view of the world.

Galbraith would not oppose the Adam Smith view explicitly as undesirable; he never does that. He would agree with every word I have just said. But if he were here he would say:

> *Ah, but you're a visionary. That's unrealistic. That isn't the way the world really is. Technical development and technical growth have made it essential that we have these large corporations and these large governments and these large organisations. And therefore your picture is a dream, a Utopia that is incapable of achievement.*

That is a claim which I believe the various critics of Galbraith have shown to be unfounded. These large enterprises are in practice not large relative to the market as a whole, not any larger than they were a hundred years ago. Large governments are not produced, and have not been produced, by technical necessities making things occur on a larger scale. There is no technical necessity arising out of technological development that requires an expansion of welfare programmes, of rent controls, of government housing, of public health. Not one of these reflects technological pressure.

They reflect rather an erroneous approach of trying to use *political* methods to achieve good objectives. The growth of government reflects rather the invisible hand in politics which works in the opposite direction from the invisible hand in economics.

In *economics* those people who attempt to pursue only their own self-interest are led by an invisible hand to promote the *public* interest.

In the *political* sphere individuals like Galbraith who attempt to pursue the public interest as they view it are led by an invisible hand to further *private* interests which it is no part of their intention to promote.

4 Questions and Answers

Easy (wrong) and difficult (right) economic thinking

QUESTION: I work in the City and the Stock Market and I have been in a university for a very long time before. The thing that really puzzles me, and while I agree with most of your views, why is it that the theories and thoughts of Professor Galbraith find so much more of an audience in the academic world than your views? And do you think that there is any change occurring?

FRIEDMAN: The answer to that is they don't. I don't mean to be in any way other than strictly factual. Galbraith's theories have never found any acceptance in the *academic* world – their acceptance has been in the *public* world. He has written for the public at large. Now I will restate your question: Why do his theories find so much more acceptance in the public world than the theories or arguments of persons like myself? And the answer is because they are much more satisfying to the ordinary man. They are easy to understand – it is easy to understand that if something is wrong there's some devil somewhere who's doing it to you. On the other hand, the kind of theories that people like me try to put across are hard to understand. This is a great defect unfortunately; it has always been one of the great difficulties of getting a market system accepted. The argument for a market is a sophisticated argument. It has to do with how a complicated system works indirectly by channels that nobody sees, by forces that have no names attached to them. That is a much harder point of view to get across than the notion that particular people are pulling levers and doing things to you. It is much harder to get across the idea that the way to cure a problem may be to allow the impersonal forces of the market to work than the idea that the way to cure something is to pass a law and appoint a minister. If you have a drought, well, you obviously appoint a Minster of Drought! The only reason why the market system has managed to survive to the extent that it has is because it is so much more efficient and effective than all of these ministers. If it were not, if the market system were not 10 times as efficient as the governmental system, all of our countries would long since have had the market completely taken over.

Let me go back, however, to your first point because I think it is very important and interesting. If someone speaks of the school of Adam Smith you can name people, academic, scientific people who are followers of Smith. If we speak of the Keynesians we can name respectable academics who have contributed to the Keynesian canon and to the Keynesian view. It is very hard to name academic people who have contributed to the Galbraithian view. It's fundamentally a one-man crusade. Go back to the philosophical radicals. That wasn't John Stuart Mill alone; there was quite a group of intellectually respectable people contributing to the argument. Whom else can you name who belongs to the Galbraithians? And I cite this as evidence to support my answer to your question, that you are confusing a popular reaction with an academic and intellectual reaction.

Inflation in Chile

QUESTION: ... Have the policies of the present government in Chile been successful in curing inflation?

FRIEDMAN: Well, that has very little to do with John Kenneth Galbraith but I'll be glad to answer it. In the first place let me make one point clear. I have not been guiding the economic policies of Chile! I have not known over the past year or so whether to be more flattered or amused by the powers which have been attributed to me. I spent six days a year ago (in April 1975) in Chile and have had no contact since with anybody in Chile and yet I am given credit for guiding the day-to-day policies of that government. But let me say the answer to your question is that, first of all, the government of Chile has not followed a severely deflationary policy; they have reduced the rate of growth of the money supply from something over 20 per cent a month to something in the neighbourhood of 10 per cent a month. Now that's a sharp reduction and that has been accompanied by a reduction in the rate of inflation from something over 20 per cent a month to something under 10 per cent a month. So as I understand it – all of this is secondhand, I have not studied the recent statistics myself, but I have talked with people who are experts on the Chilean situation – the evidence seems to be that there has been a sharp reduction in the rate of inflation as a result of a sharp reduction in the rate of monetary growth; this result followed with a much shorter lag of course than it would here.

As you know, in the United States and the United Kingdom there has over the past hundred years been about a two-year lag between changes in the money supply and changes in prices. That's not a fact of nature, but a result of our both having systems which had relatively stable prices over fairly long periods. In countries like Chile or Brazil or Argentina and the like the lag is much shorter; a change in the money supply is followed within a few months by the appropriate price changes because people have been much more attuned to wide fluctuations in the rate of inflation. Now, as I understand the Chilean situation, the initial relatively deflationary policies did have the expected consequences both of a reduction in the rate of inflation and an initial reduction in output and employment. In addition, the government undertook to cut down government spending, to privatise enterprises, putting them back into private hands, to free foreign exchange.

As I understand it, there has been a very rapid improvement in non-traditional exports and in the foreign balance of payments. I am told that the major source of the increases in the money supply in the past year have come from the necessity of raising funds to pay off foreign debts. The output in agriculture has increased very rapidly in the past two years, industrial output has fallen and industrial unemployment rose in Santiago, but there has been a turn and the indices of production and employment are now going up.

Will Galbraith come true?

QUESTION: Will Galbraith's view be the view of the future?

FRIEDMAN: No. The future may be a technostructure, but if so it will be a government collectivist technostructure and not a private industry technostructure. The great danger of the Galbraithian view is precisely that it stresses the importance, from his point of view, of an expansion in the role of government. Unfortunately, while he would like to see that governmental rôle be carried through by disinterested intellectuals, it will not be. It will be carried through by very highly interested bureaucrats, and they will run the society from the centre as such societies have always tended to be run: as collectivist societies which reduce and greatly limit the freedom of individuals.

There are two different questions. What is *likely* to happen and what *can* happen; what *needs* to happen, what is *possible*. Many of the large aggregations of enterprise, I would argue, have arisen from bad government policy and not from technological necessity. In my country, about which I can speak much more confidently than I can about yours, our tax system has established a very strong pressure toward merger and conglomeration of enterprises. Governmental control and regulation in industries such as the power industry, the telephone industry, the communications industry, the aircraft industry, have made for large enterprises. The most obvious example is aircraft. Since the Civil Aeronautics Board started to exercise control over air carriers, in the 1930s, not a single new trunk line has been approved, and the number of major trunk lines in the United States is smaller today than it was in 1938. And this is not for want of applicants – there have been many applicants. If we could abolish the Civil Aeronautics Board tomorrow, there is no doubt whatsoever that our aircraft industry would be in an extremely healthy state, with a very much larger number of enterprises and very much less concentration of power. The same is true in the broadcasting and television industry. Why do we have three major networks? Because the Federal Communications Commission has prevented competition in television and radio. It has held back the introduction of pay TV, of cable TV, of every new invention. If we could abolish the Federal Communications Commission tomorrow and auction off the right to the various channels and so on, there is no doubt that in a very short period we would have a much larger number of very effective and efficient television companies. And so it goes in industry after industry.

The relationship between size and government control, in my opinion, is the reverse of that which Galbraith presents. He presents a picture in which the large enterprises grow and then take the government in to help them plan. Now there is no doubt that business enterprises will in fact *try* to use the government for their purposes and often are successful in doing so. Adam Smith wrote that two centuries ago. But the relationship in the United States has been that government measures have promoted the concentration of industry and the growth of large enterprises; and in the absence of the government measures that need not have happened at all. So I don't think there is any necessity for the Galbraithian picture, either for the present or for the future.

But I very much fear that we may develop in the direction of an increasingly bureaucratised, collectivist, socialist kind of society – that is the direction in which Britain is going. If I am an English businessman the sensible thing for me to do is to make large losses, provided I can counterpoise those losses with an accumulation of foreign exchange somewhere. Then the government will come in and bail me out of my losses and buy me out. This is a way in which British industry has been increasingly taken over by your government, which has been borrowing foreign exchange abroad to enable people at home to get their money out. Now it's a good thing that people should be able to get their money out: I am not in favour of exchange control, I think it ought to be abolished, but I'm only describing the process that has been going on and why I think that you're moving in that direction rather than the other direction. It's an interesting thing that one of Galbraith's major points, one on which Sir Frank McFadzean particularly attacked him correctly, was in saying 'Oh, these big enterprises never make losses.' Now you can hardly think of any prophecy which has been more convincingly contradicted by the experience in the United States and Britain.

Motive and consequence in economic policy

QUESTION: What empirical evidence is there for the good intentions of the reformers?

FRIEDMAN: The question is very interesting. I have to admit I have no answer. However, I do not believe it is a crucial point. The important point is a different one.

I said that there was an invisible hand in the political sphere whereby those well-meaning people who attempted to use the political mechanism to do good were led to serve private interests that they would never voluntarily have served. On the whole it seems to me very unsatisfactory to attack issues by trying to question what people's *motives* are. That gets you into a morass. First of all, an argument may be right or wrong regardless of the motives of the person who presented it. The person may have presented a self-interested argument – that does not mean it is wrong. The important question is: What are the *consequences* of the way people behave and act? And the only point I would make is – for the moment let's grant complete disinterest on the part of the people, let's grant the best of intentions. What would be the consequences? And would it really be true that the bad consequences of these measures follow from the bad intentions, or would those bad consequences follow even if people had good intentions? The reply I would give is that even if people had the very best of intentions – and I don't question their motives – the evil consequences that we have seen would still follow. Why?

Economic versus political markets

The reason is the fundamental difference between an economic mechanism and a political mechanism. The fundamental difference is that in the economic market you get what you pay for. In the political market you do not get what you vote for. Now that's a very fundamental difference in its simplest terms. If in the economic market I go to spend a dollar I am going to get a dollar's worth and therefore I have a dollar's worth of incentive to make sure I spend that dollar well. If I go to vote in the political market, at most mine is one of a thousand votes and I'm not going to get what I vote for, I'm going to get what 51 per cent of the people vote for. And therefore in general *I have no incentive to vote intelligently.*

Suppose I am asked to vote on the question of whether there should be a tariff on shoes, or indirectly whether my representative should vote for it. How much money is it worth my spending to inform myself on that issue? The answer is one cent, or two cents. On the other hand, the manufacturers of shoes are in a different situation: their interests are concentrated; that particular measure (the tariff) means a great deal to them. It will be worth their while to spend a good deal getting that measure passed. That is why it is in the political self-interest of people in politics to create and serve a coalition of special interests rather than a general interest. In the same way let people, with the best intentions in the world, legislate a measure. Who has any incentive to keep tabs on what happens to it after it's voted? The public at large is led to believe that poor people are getting cheated in their housing and so they vote for rent control. But once the rent control authority is established, in whose interest is it run? And this goes on over and over again – the Inter-State Commerce Commission, the FDA, whatever you want to name. The political process is one which has an invisible hand in the sense that *it is against the private interest to vote in the public interest.* And therefore *you cannot have a political mechanism which will in practice achieve the sum of the general public interest as the market does.*

I haven't really answered your question – I'm not sure I can – but do let me urge that we will do much better if we don't get ourselves involved in calling names or questioning motives but take people for what they profess to be. After all, we're asking them to do that to us!

One of the great puzzles is how to explain the growth of this kind of intervention. This is the question we started with. And another kind of an answer is that for many of us it is in our self-interest to be in favour of intervention. Certainly for economists, there is nothing that produces jobs for economists like government controls and government intervention. And all economists are therefore schizophrenic: their discipline, derived from Adam Smith, leads them to favour the market; their self-interest leads them to favour intervention. And in large part the profession has been led to reconcile these two opposing forces by being in favour of the market in general but opposed to it in particular. We are very clever at finding 'special cases' – there are external effects, there are monopolies, there are imperfections in the market; therefore we can have our cake and eat it. We can be in favour of the free market and we can at the same time promote those separate interventions that promote our private interest by providing jobs for economists.

II The Road to Economic Freedom: the Steps from Here to There

5 Introduction

Before we start on the discussion I cannot resist informing some of you, and Arthur Seldon[18] in particular, that there are some respects in which American trade unions are worse than British trade unions. I have just discovered one this afternoon, in taping a brief comment for the BBC. In the United States if a gentleman like Terence Kelly[19] came around to interview me with a cassette tape recorder and one side of the cassette tape ran out and he had to turn it over, that cassette would be wiped out when he got back to the office because it is the function of a technician, not of a reporter, to turn the cassette over. And so he has to be sure that he can record everything on one side of the cassette! But here in Britain I saw Terence here – and this is a tape recorder rather than a cassette recorder – actually put in a new tape! Now that surely is a job for a technician! Now why is that? Because the trade unions don't think there's enough fat in the BBC to go after? What the reason is, I don't know, but at any rate you'll be glad to know that you've got some advantages.

Getting from here to there

We need to divide the major question 'from here to there' into two very different issues. One has to do with the problem of how you get out of the kind of situation in which Britain now is, with something like 60 per cent of the national income being spent by government, and with an inflation which has gone up and down for years. How you turn that situation around and get the basic economic structure of the economy into a healthy situation is one class of problem. There is a second and very different class of problem: how do you unwind the various social welfare or industrial intervention measures that your government undertakes? The first is a problem of general financial policy and the second of detailed social and economic policy.

6 The Immediate Financial Task

The first of these is in some ways the immediate problem that a country like Britain is faced with. Suppose you had the will, which you haven't, how should you go about trying to get the economy on to a healthy basis?

Gradualism

Now in this particular issue I believe that one major question is gradualism versus shock treatment. That is a question to which the same answer cannot be given under all circumstances. If you are in the situation of the United States today, with an inflation rate running at about 6 per cent a year, total governmental spending at about 40 per cent of the national income – in which we have been getting worse but are at a much less advanced state of the disease than you are – I am all in favour of a very gradual return to a non-inflationary position. I would not be in favour of trying to get a zero rate of inflation next year because there are all sorts of contracts people have entered into, including borrowing and lending contracts at rates of interest that implicitly allow for a considerable measure of inflation. There are employment contracts, building contracts, and so on, and it would be very disturbing to the arrangements voluntarily reached amongst individuals if you were overnight to go from, say, 6 per cent to zero. I think in the United States it would be desirable to go to zero over a period of four or five years, by cutting down the rate of inflation by about 1 per cent per year. Personally I would like to see that policy announced in advance so that people could adjust themselves to it. And I would call that a relatively gradual approach to a state of financial equilibrium.

Shock treatment

On the other hand, to take the extreme opposite case: a year ago I was in Chile which was faced with the problem of an inflation of 20 per cent a *month*. Now that is a different story altogether. To talk about that country trying to reduce its inflation rate at the rate of 1 per cent a year is silly. A country in that position has very few long-term contracts. One of the major effects of such a rapid rate of inflation is that people do not engage in long-term contracts which are contingent upon what the rate of inflation is going to be. Liquid resources are very small. Total money supply in Chile at that time amounted to three days' payment. It's a hand-to-mouth situation of the most extreme kind, because of course if prices are going up at 20 per cent a month you are going to make arrangements to keep to a very minimum the amount of cash or non-interest-earning assets you hold. And under those circumstances it seemed to me, as I argued then, as I would now, that the only sensible thing to do is a shock treatment, in which you make a very sharp move. You cut the figure right away and try to bring the inflation rate down to your long-term objective in a very short period.

These are not only hypothetical questions. We have a good deal of historical experience. There are two very important episodes in recent decades which illustrate how effective a shock treatment of that kind can be. One is the German Erhard episode in 1948, when Erhard terminated all wage and price controls over one weekend. He did it on a Sunday because the American, British, and French occupation offices were closed and they would not be able to countermand his orders! A very similar situation occurred in Japan about the same time, in response to a mission from the United States headed by a banker from Detroit by the name of Dodge. The Japanese again used essentially shock treatment of a monetary reform, substituting a new money under new circumstances, cutting government spending sharply, getting the government's budget into a more tolerable position. In both cases you had very favourable results. Of course there were unfavourable aspects of the immediate shock, but they lasted only a short period, because you did not have long-term contracts built into the system that are the major source of difficulty in unwinding a high inflation.

Chile and Britain

In Chile they engaged in a shock treatment but only went halfway. They cut the growth of the money supply from something over 20 per cent a *month* to something over 10 per cent a month and brought the inflation rate down from 20 per cent a month to 10 per cent a month. I was very interested in the Chilean case because certain of the fundamental parameters were almost identical with those of the British case. The government deficit in Chile, which was being financed by printing money, was about 10 per cent of the national income. At that time the British government deficit, or borrowing requirement, was also roughly 10 per cent of the national income.

The reason why you are able to get away with so much lower an inflation rate of 20 per cent a *year* instead of 20 per cent a *month* is, first, that you are in a position to borrow half of that from overseas. Chile was not. Secondly, you did not have the long background of inflation as a result of which the Chileans had reduced their money holding to such small totals as three days' spending. In the United Kingdom you had a much larger total of liquid assets, so that inflation was a very much more productive tax in the United Kingdom than in Chile. To finance a budget deficit equal to 5 per cent of the national income by printing money thus required an inflation tax of only 20 or 25 per cent a year, and not 20 per cent a month as in Chile. But if Britain were to continue along these lines, those advantages would disappear, and you would be unable to borrow abroad. The tax would become progressively a less productive source of revenue, and to finance similar deficits you would have to engage in ever higher levels of inflation.

Modified shock treatment for Britain

The British case is not the American case and it is not the Chilean, German or Japanese cases – it is in between. And yet I think it is far enough along the way towards the German, Japanese or Chilean cases to make Britain a good candidate for a shock treatment, and not for a very gradualistic approach to cutting inflation at a slow rate over a long period. By shock treatment again I do not mean it would be feasible for you to bring the rate of inflation down to zero next month. But I see no reason why you should not try to establish guidelines and policies which would bring you into a roughly zero inflation within something like three to five years.

The instruments

What is required in order to do that? What do I mean by a shock treatment? The shock treatment can work in the British case if, and only if, it enables Britain to cut down the amount of money it has to create to finance its obligations. How can it do that?

Number one, and most importantly, you must cut government spending. I have no doubt that the absolute *sine qua non* of a non-inflationary policy in Britain is a cut. I do *not* mean a cut in the prospective *increase*; I mean a real cut in government spending and a cut that is substantial. That is the first requisite. Look at your figures now. You are spending something like 60 per cent of the national income through the government. Your explicit taxes are raising at most something like 50 per cent of the national income, and then only with systems of taxes which have severe disincentive effects on working, saving, and investing. The first step has to be to eliminate the need to finance that 10 per cent. That means a very minimum objective is to cut government spending from 60 down to 50 per cent of national income – something like that – within three years.

You could go further than that. The cut in government spending by a sixth is not a major magnitude. It would not reduce efficiency. There is little doubt that if you were to go through every government bureau in the United Kingdom and fire every sixth man, the productivity of the other five would go up rather than down. Your own experience of a three-day week in industry in February 1974 was very impressive evidence from that point of view. But the *political* difficulty is of course very severe, because the immediate initial effect of such cutting looks as if it is adding to unemployment. It is really not adding to unemployment. Rather it is rendering people available for *productive* employment instead of *unproductive* employment. Most of those people would be absorbed in a fairly brief period.

In any event, the only question that arises is: How can you cut government spending by that much? I have come to a very simple conclusion. There is only one way to do it. It is *not* by looking for places where money is wasted, *not* by seeking the worst workplaces, but *across the board*. You have to do it by saying: every department, every office is going to have a statutory obligation to make cuts year by year. It seems to me the only way to cut that is feasible is to say that this year every office, every department, is to be cut by 10 per cent; next year it is to be cut by another 10 per cent; and the year after that by another 10 per cent. And only then do you arrange the cuts as you will within departments. Only then can you consider the special case and have each department fight with every other department for a change in that total allocation. But once you start along the lines 'We're going to find waste', you will find that it is universal and then you open the door to the special interest behind each particular activity to bring their full pressure to bear; and you are then back in the whole story of special interest politics.

The public at large, I think, is much more likely to support a policy – indeed it has begun to support a policy – that says 'We are going to cut government spending from 60 per cent of the national income to 50 per cent in the next two or three years, and we are going to do it across the board.' If you start arguing with the public at large, by saying, 'We can get rid of a little bit of this department' or 'There's a wasteful activity here', it will be hopeless to get backing for it. That seems to me, from an economic point of view, to be the sensible way to go about your cuts in government spending.

Tax system reform by shock treatment

The second requisite of course is to re-organise the tax structure. Here again I think you really need a shock treatment and not a gradual move in one direction or another. There is nobody in your country or mine who does not recognise that our present tax system is a mess. It does not in practice achieve any of the objectives claimed for it. It taxes people who are in the same position differently, depending on the source of their income and on the accident of whether they can escape the tax.

One of the striking things that always seems a paradox to people from overseas who come to visit Britain is that they are puzzled as to why there are so many Rolls-Royces in a country on the verge of destruction, in which productivity has been going downhill, in which you have had great inefficiency, and in which the government has been dedicated these many years to egalitarianism. How come all these Rolls-Royces? And then you see the prices charged for second-hand Rolls-Royces. How can these people afford to pay £10,000, £20,000 for Rolls-Royces? The answer is very simple, as you know better than anybody else. It is the *cheapest* way in the world for anybody who has wealth to try to conserve it and also to buy transportation. If the alternative to investing that wealth in a Rolls-Royce is to invest it in income-yielding securities, most of the income is going to go to the tax collector, whereas it does not cost anything to have a Rolls-Royce. A man invests, say, £30,000 in a Rolls-Royce. If he invested it in income-earning securities, earning, say, 15 per cent, he would get a gross yield of £4,500 a year. If he's in the 98 per cent tax bracket he has only £90 a year left after tax to spend. So it costs him only £90 a year to have his Rolls-Royce all year! It's the cheapest form of transportation he can possibly buy! In addition, he has the advantage of an asset that will conserve some of its capital value. If he put it in government bonds, then every year it is going to be worth less, even aside from the amount that the government takes from him in taxes. And so your tax system discourages saving and investment. *It encourages wasteful, 'conspicuous' consumption.*

Again, if I ask what it costs an employer to employ a man, on the one hand, and what is the net yield to a man from being employed, on the other, I find both in your country and mine the tax system has introduced a very large wedge. I do not understand why people are puzzled by the phenomenon of simultaneous higher unemployment benefit and lower employment. Economic principles work: if you increase the demand for anything, the supply will grow to meet it. In your country and mine we have made it ever more attractive to be unemployed. *We have increased the demand for unemployment,* and the supply of unemployed has risen to meet that demand. On the other hand, we have imposed a heavy tax on employing anyone. So the result is that we have made employers unwilling to employ people. The wedge between the cost to the employer and the net return to the employee has become bigger and bigger.

Indexation and lower tax rates

I know what I would say in the United States, but I do not know enough of the British tax system to assess how I would go about reconstructing it in Britain. But I do know what the essential features are: first, index-ation of the tax system so as to eliminate the tendency for inflation to push people up into ever-higher brackets and to eliminate the temptation for governments to use inflation as a way of financing their business. Secondly, a reduction in the special allowances and a sharp reduction along with that in the marginal rate of tax. You can raise the present revenue at vastly *lower* taxes if you apply the tax rates to the *whole* of the income, however earned and received, with no tax-free allowances. In the United States we have tax rates that go from 14 per cent at the bottom to 70 per cent at the top. You have rates which go up much higher than that. But if you eliminated the special deductions, exemptions and so-called loopholes from the income tax in the United States, you could raise the same revenue with the same personal exemptions with,

I think, a flat rate of around 16 per cent. And in practice you would raise a lot more than that.

In a column I wrote a year or so ago[20] I demonstrated pretty conclusively, I think, that the United States government would get more revenue than it now gets from the personal income tax if it made no change in the law except to replace all tax rates above 25 per cent by 25 per cent. That change would yield *more* revenue because it would make it unprofitable for people to resort to the tax gimmicks and loopholes they now use. *They would report more revenue.* The taxpayer would be better off and the Exchequer would be better off. One of the great mistakes people make in taxation policy is to treat the tax receipts of the government as if they corresponded to the cost of the taxes to the taxpayer. They do not. Because of the existence of the tax system, taxpayers are led to do all sorts of things (in the form of tax avoidance or evasion, including not working or engaging in occupations different from those they would engage in if taxes were lower) that are very costly to them but which yield no revenue to the government. It is this difference between the total cost to the taxpayer and the total receipts to the government that offers the opportunity for reductions that will benefit both the revenue and the taxpayer. This is the second shock treatment you badly need in the sense of a very substantial modification and change in the tax system.

I have only one other thing to say on how you get back to a non-inflationary state. I think it is right to put emphasis on how you hold down the quantity of money, but I think it is wrong to suppose that it is some kind of simple cure that can be introduced without affecting anything else. The real problem is to adjust the budget and government expenditures in such a way that it is feasible to hold down the rate of growth of the quantity of money.

7 Unwinding Government

Now let us suppose by some miracle you really had a political régime that was committed to moving away from the kind of welfare state, nationalised apparatus that Britain has, and that the US has been increasingly moving towards, and wanted to get to a largely free enterprise state in which people had a good deal more leeway about how they handled their own resources than they have now. What general principles can you think of that are relevant in proceeding from here to there?

Denationalisation by auctioning or giving away

Once again in some cases it is appropriate to get rid of it all at once. Most of these cases have to do with nationalisation of economic activities. I do not see any sense in saying 'We are going to "privatise" the steel industry piece meal' or 'We are going to sell off to the public 1 per cent of the steel industry each year'. The obvious thing to do with the steel industry, the railroads, and all those industries currently governmentally operated is to get rid of them by auctioning them off. Here there are various devices. At the moment it would be very hard to auction off the steel industry, because a Tory government did it once and then a Labour government renationalised it and anybody who buys it again would now be very uncertain that he would be able to retain ownership. One suggestion a number of people have made which I think makes a great deal of sense would be, not to auction it off, but to give it away, by giving every citizen in the country a share in it.

After all, the supposed argument is that the people of Great Britain own the steel industry; it is the property of all the citizens. Well, then, why not give each citizen his piece? Now you may say this raises some questions of feasibility. You might say 55 million shares are a lot of shares – in order to have a market in them you would have to re-introduce the farthing to enable people to buy and sell them. That's true.

A mutual fund

But it seems to me you could go at it in a very different way. You have not only the steel industry, but electricity, the BBC, railroads, road transport, etc. Suppose you constructed a mutual fund to which you assigned the shares in all these enterprises and then gave every one of the 55 million citizens of the United Kingdom a share in it. Now you are talking about magnitudes that are perfectly feasible.

I do not think individuals would regard a share in such a fund as derisory. And I do not see why that really is not the kind of approach you want to adopt because it meets every socialist value. These enterprises belong to the people; so we are going to give them to the people. This method has a big advantage. If you tried to auction these industries off individually, the *government* would get the revenue and it would waste it. But if you give it to the *people*, and you allow a market to be established, you would see in a very short period that this would unsnarl itself. In the first place, individuals would start to buy and sell the mutual shares they were given. In the second place, the mutual enterprise would see a market starting to be established in its stock. Perhaps you would need three or four mutuals. I am not going into details; I am trying to get at the principles. The fundamental principle is to do it in a way which gives the public at large a strong incentive to have it done, and not in a way which is simply another channel for the government to acquire revenue, as for example the UK government did in selling off the steel industry in the first place and then renationalising it. I think that kind of unwinding ought to be done all at once.

Towards profitability

But what if most of these industries now make a loss? They would not, once they were liberated from government control. You accomplish two purposes at once: you reduce the governmental deficit at the same time as you provide for a more efficient private economy. It may be reasonable, in 'privatising' them – in giving them to the mutual fund – for Parliament to provide a guarantee of a year or two of subsidy to enable them to get on their feet.

Let us leave aside the political issue and examine the economic issue. Suppose I say I want to auction off the steel industry. It may be that its market price as now nationalised is negative. Therefore the auction procedure might be for the government to say: 'Who will take the steel industry off our hands for the least subsidy?' And similarly with the mutual fund. But from a political point of view it seems to me far more preferable to distribute it amongst the public at large than to try to do it by paying somebody to take it off your hands. And if the trade unions object, then give the nationalised industries to the unions.

8 Reduction of Government by Gradualism

Now I want to go on to the other class of policies where you need to proceed more gradually. These are the classic cases in which you have a government that has put individuals in a position where they are dependent on government bounty and in which you cannot really throw them out overnight. As a result of the welfare state measures that your country and my country have undertaken, millions of people today are dependent on the bounty of the state for their livelihood, and you cannot simply say we are going to cut that off overnight and throw them out on the street. The question here is, then, different. How do you set up arrangements which will simultaneously enable you to wind down those programmes but at the same time do not create great difficulties for settled expectations?

Vouchers or cash

Here I think the one principle which can be applied is that in general you can do so by trying to substitute vouchers or cash payments for services in kind or vouchers for particular groups in place of across-the-board payments and subsidies to everybody.

The voucher scheme has received perhaps most attention in education. Certainly it is, in my opinion, about the only feasible way to go from the government-dominated educational system we now have to the kind under which you have a free, competitive private-market educational system. That would be desirable. The virtues of the voucher system are in my opinion two-fold. One is that it introduces choice and enables competition to come into effect. That is the virtue that has been most discussed. But for the moment I want to discuss another virtue of a very different kind.

This is the possibility of winding things down, of reducing the fraction of the total costs borne by the government and thereby returning activities to the private sector. Ask anybody the abstract question: Is the case for governmental provision of education stronger in a poor society or in an affluent society? Or, is it more appropriate to expect parents to pay for the schooling of their children in a poor country or in a rich country? Almost everybody will answer: 'Obviously in a rich country it is more appropriate for parents to pay and there is more of a case for governmental provision in a poor country.' And yet *historically the relationship has been the other way round*.

In your country and my country, as we have become richer, the fraction of total educational expenditure that is borne by the state has gone *up*. Why? I believe the major reason is that governments have financed education through running educational *institutions*. They have set up schools and run them and therefore there has been no way in which private individuals could spend private money in a marginal way. As societies became more affluent people at large wanted to spend more on education but, given that government was providing the education, that led to more *government* provision.

Now one of the great virtues of a voucher system is that it makes it possible to move in the other direction. If you have a voucher of a fixed dollar or pound value, as the society gets richer people are encouraged to add to it, to use private provision in a marginal way to improve the kind of education and schooling their children get. You can think of the fraction of total governmental education expenditure declining over time so long as you can hold back the political pressures to raise the value of the vouchers. The political pressure then would not have only one place to go; it could at least be diverted by the opportunity to supplement state provision. Perhaps it would not in fact be diverted, but if you have a people committed to getting back to a free society it seems to me that is one of the great virtues of using vouchers.

Reverse income tax

The same thing goes for housing vouchers or medical vouchers. And of course it goes in a far more fundamental sense for eliminating the specific kinds of vouchers and getting a general voucher in the form of a reverse income tax. Now again, one of the virtues of a reverse income tax – (I once labelled it as a 'negative income tax' but the British use 'reverse income tax'. I must say I think negative income tax is more accurate because a negative tax is a subsidy but a reverse tax is – I don't know what a reverse tax is. Anyway, call it what you will.)[21] – its great virtue is that you do not have a system under which you provide medical care by special provision *in kind*, or provide housing and schooling by special services, and so on. In the first place you need a bureaucracy to administer each of these services and this establishes a very, very strong pressure for their maintenance and extension. I think it is true that the greatest forces in your country and in mine which have been promoting an extension of governmental welfare measures have not been the demand from the public at large, or the pressure of well-meaning reformers, but the internal pressure to extend the civil service to administer it.

I do not know how many people in Britain have read Pat Moynihan's book on the family assistance plan in the United States,[22] on the problems that arose when Mr Nixon at one stage proposed what was essentially a negative income tax. The theme of Moynihan's book is that that proposal was largely defeated by the welfare bureaucracy. They were the ones who really stirred up the trouble and defeated the proposal.[23] Look at it the other way: if you can put through a negative income tax as a *substitute* for, not an *addition* to, all the special piecemeal programmes, it has the great virtue that it will enable you to reduce the bureaucracy and reduce this pressure. And it also offers some hope that over a period you can gradually reduce the extent to which the government provides, e.g. schooling, as opposed to private provision.

The transition: special cases

One final point on the problem of the transition: in the United States we have tried to work in some detail on some of the special cases – social security, schooling, housing and so on. I cannot really do that for Britain but I think there are two fundamental principles: first, use the market mechanisms as much as you can in turning back the special provisions in kind; second, introduce gradualism of a type which can be made self-destructive.

Let me stop there and deal with anything you want to talk about.

9 Questions and Answers

Cutting transfer payments

QUESTION: On the last point Professor Friedman made about welfare payments: much of the government's 60 per cent of the GNP is transfer payments, i.e. cash subsidies from the social rich to the social poor. And if we make a 10 per cent cut in government spending, where are you going to cut the subsidies the recipients get? You can't get it from the bureaucracy, anyway in the short term; you may in the long term. Would you say you should preserve their value in the short term while trying to introduce the voucher or the reverse tax – we call it the tax credit now – in which case, of course, the bulk of the cuts is going to fall all the more heavily on other programmes like roads.

FRIEDMAN: No, I would not preserve the real value of transfer payments. If you can think of substituting a negative income tax it would cost far less than it costs you now if you replace your unemployment and health insurance arrangements, and so on, and bundle all of them together. The point is that all of the money you are now spending on transfer payments is not going to the poor. On the contrary, a lot of it is going to people who are not poor, and one of the main reasons is the proliferation of separate benefits. There is somebody who qualifies independently for benefits A,B,C,D, and E, and by the time you add them all together he is getting much more than anybody would think it appropriate to provide. So I think it is admirably appropriate to cut down spending on transfer payments.

Incidentally, I was not suggesting a cut of 10 per cent of government spending, but a cut of 10 per cent of the national income, which is a cut of 17 per cent on government spending, not 10 per cent. The aim is to bring government spending down from 60 per cent of the national income to 50 per cent. But I see no reason why that should not come in part out of the so-called transfer payments.

The cost of vouchers

MARJORIE SELDON: I'm often asked how you reconcile the need to cut government spending with the voucher system because if you give the voucher to every child the cost would be notionally about £140 million for the 5, 6 or 7 per cent of children educated privately. So you are, they say, adding to public expenditure.

FRIEDMAN: I have always answered that objection by saying I am going to calculate the size of the voucher by taking total current spending on schooling and dividing it by the *total* number of schoolchildren. I know from comparisons that the cost of private schooling, given comparable qualities, is roughly *half* the cost of the state system. Indeed, I may say this is a very interesting phenomenon. There is a sort of empirical generalisation that *it costs the state twice as much to do anything as it costs private enterprise,* whatever it is. My son[24] once called my attention to this generalisation, and it is amazing how accurate it is. Some studies have been done in the United States on the productivity in handling accounts of people in the governmental social security system and in the private insurance system and private commercial insurance agencies and, lo and behold, the ratio of productivity was 2 : 1. There are some cities and States in the United States which provide private profit-making fire departments; in Scottsdale, Arizona, for example, there is a private free enterprise fire department that protects citizens against fire by charging for it. And it turns out that it costs them half as much as it costs the municipal fire-fighting department. I don't want to overstate the exact 2 : 1 ratio, but roughly that is what it is. In schools there is no doubt that there is at least a 2 : 1 difference. So if you took the total amount of money now being spent, divided it by the total number of children to get it, you do not add anything to expenditure. You would cut the voucher sums available to pupils in government schools by this 5 or 10 per cent, or whatever it is. But with that lower amount they could buy far *better* schooling than they are getting now, so everybody would be better off.

Experiment with vouchers

MRS SELDON: Would you advocate experiment? You might not get the response of the market because people would say it's temporary and might come to an end. So you would not get the kind of responses you would have if you introduced it nationally. Would you therefore introduce it generally rather than in limited areas?

FRIEDMAN: I do not believe that is a question to be answered in the abstract. I think it is not going to be politically feasible to get it adopted overall unless it has been tried out in an experiment. I grant you an experiment will not be as satisfactory as a real commitment to it. But I would certainly be in favour of experiment because, again, if you were talking about a system that was going to be only 5 per cent better than another system, the difficulties of the experiment you point out would be very serious. But you are talking about a system that is going to be twice as efficient as the state system. So you can afford to have an *imperfect* experiment and still have very striking and effective results. Moreover, if you have an experiment for a five- or six-year period, it turns out that schooling does not require very long-term capital investment. You have had people setting up schools on a very temporary basis. So I think you would be surprised at the extent of the reaction you would get to an experiment. Unfortunately we have not been able to have a very good experiment in the United States so we do not have very much evidence for you.

Political intervention with a voucher system

STEPHEN EYRES: I was beginning to have second thoughts on vouchers and negative income tax as a way of introducing or restoring markets into hitherto state-provided areas because, although a market-oriented government may introduce a voucher system, this would not stop interventionist politicians imposing interventionist solutions to voucher schemes, such as advocating compensatory vouchers for specific interest groups or geographical areas. If we propose to phase out the vouchers over a period of time, the trouble is that people do not like having benefits taken away from them, and politicians could propose that the state part of the finance should be increased and not decreased.

FRIEDMAN: There are those problems, of course. The question is: What is the alternative? In higher education, I am 100 per cent with you. I think the right thing to do is to have loans: no doubt about that. But we are now talking about universal elementary and secondary education. I do not think fees-with-lower-taxes meets the political problems you are raising. On the contrary, I think it exacerbates them, because it very much encourages the introduction of fees in accordance with income. It encourages the use of fees as a supplementary method of taxing income, which is the counterpart of your compensatory voucher arrangement.

You are not solving the political problem by a fees-with-lower-taxes arrangement. If anything, you are making it more severe; and, so long as the state runs the schools, so long as taxes are used to subsidise the schools *per se*, you have no in-built mechanism to create a counter-move. You see, one of the virtues of the voucher system is that, insofar as it encourages private schools, it tends to build up a special group that has an interest in continuing the voucher system as opposed to going to state-supported schools. But you lose that advantage if you go the way of fees-with-lower-taxes.

Countering the 'vote motive'

CHRISTOPHER TAME: What is to prevent the politicians vying with each other to increase the monetary value of the vouchers?

FRIEDMAN: There's nothing to prevent that. And that raises a supplementary question of a different kind which I should have mentioned earlier. How do you prevent, or how do you act in such a way as to avoid, the 'vote motive'?[25] There is only one way I have seen that avoids it at all, and that is by somehow having a very strong public commitment to *aggregate* as opposed to *individual* items. You see, the big way in which the vote motive operates, the defect of the political system, is that there is a tendency for each individual group to try to get its own way at the expense of the community at large. And so the special interest groups have a common interest in attacking the public at large.

There is one device we have been trying to work out in the United States that has been receiving wide attention. We of course have a written constitution, which you do not. We have tried to institute constitutional provisions setting a limit to the maximum amount of money as a fraction of the national income that governments may spend in all directions. Governor Reagan in California a couple of years ago sponsored Proposition I, which was to be an amendment to the State of California constitution. It was to limit State spending to the same percentage of the State income as it was then, with gradual reduction in that percentage over time. It failed at adoption by a rather narrow margin, something like 47 to 53 per cent. A similar provision is going to be on the ballot in Michigan this Fall as an amendment to the Michigan constitution. In three or four other States a movement along this line is under way. In addition, a number of Congressmen have introduced proposals for a Federal constitutional amendment along these lines, and a committee of the Southern Governors Conference has been assigned to work on this problem and has prepared a constitutional amendment to the Federal constitution along this line and it is going to try to get the backing of Southern Governors for it.

The problem is that the only way you can beat the vote motive is by generally accepted limitations on the scope of government. They can be written constitutional limitations or unwritten limitations, as they are in the UK. That is what limited the scope of government in the 19th century in both our countries. I think it is very difficult to conceive of doing it now by limiting the *activities* governments can engage in, but it is still feasible to do it by limiting total government *spending*. What you need is to be able to do something which in the first place wraps together all the particular difficulties for individuals into one big whole, generalises them and enables you to achieve something by a one-time crusade and does not require eternal vigilance.

That is the great virtue in the United States of being able to get a constitutional amendment. Once you get it through, it is difficult to overturn, and you do not have to keep working at it all the time. You in Britain do not have that possibility. If, for example, we in the United States could get a constitutional amendment limiting total federal government spending, let us say, to 25 per cent of the national income, *you force the special interest groups to fight one another.*

Evidence on effectiveness (speed) of changes

QUESTION: On your point about what is necessary to move resources from unproductive units to productive units, have you any evidence at all on the rate at which that shift is feasibly possible?

FRIEDMAN: If you look at the kind of cases I was quoting, the most extreme where this was done in one fell swoop were the German and Japanese. The initial position had become very bad and this was the kind of case that Ralph Harris was citing earlier[26] about the short-term pessimists who think it has to get worse before it gets better. But it is remarkable how rapid the recovery was, on a very broad scale, both in Japan and in Germany. I am under the impression that Britain is in a position where you can have an equally rapid improvement, and that is because you are so bad now. In Britain before World War II, real income per head was double that in Germany and France, but today real income per head in Germany and France is double that in Britain. You can make very rapid progress under any circumstances where there is a large gap between your position and that of other similar countries. The reason why Japan was able to have such a very rapid rate of growth over so long a period – and more recently that has been true of Brazil as well – is that the initial level from which she started was so much lower than that of other countries.

Psychological shock?

QUESTION: As in Germany, so in Japan, the crucial thing was not the mechanism but the psychological shock which altered people's attitudes to wealth and everything else. I do not see how you are going to get that psychological shock in Britain at the moment.

FRIEDMAN: Brazil perhaps will fit your case better, because there was no such psychological shock. There it was all mechanism. It was the introduction of indexation, which brought some freeing of prices plus a floating exchange rate.

Notes

1   Harvard University Press, Cambridge, Mass., 1952
2   Hamish Hamilton, 1958; Pelican Books, 1962.
3   Published under the title *American Capitalism: Concept of Countervailing Power*, Hamish Hamilton, 1952
4   *American Economic Review, Papers and Proceedings*, May 1954, pp. 7–14.
5   Pelican Books, 1969.
6   Harbinger Books, 1963; Augustus Kelley, New York, 1970.
7   Indiana University Press, 1960 (reprinted by Greenwood Press, New York, 1972).
8   [Written with David Sawers and Richard Stillerman, Macmillan, London, 1959 (2nd ed. 1969). – ED.]
9   *Ibid.*, p. 227.
10   [*Galbraith and the Planners*, Strathclyde University Press, 1968. – ED.]
11   [*Economic Fact and Fantasy: A Rejoinder to Galbraith's Reith Lectures*, Occasional Paper 14, IEA, 1967 (2nd ed. 1969). – ED.]
12   [Economics in the Industrial State – Discussion', *American Economic Review*, May 1970. – ED.]
13   ['Where is the New Industrial State?', *Economic Inquiry* (Journal of the Western Economics Association), March 1974. – ED.]
14   [Professor Robert M. Solow's critique, 'The New Industrial State, or Son of Affluence', appeared in *The Public Interest*, No. 9, 1967. Professor Galbraith's reply, in the same issue, was entitled 'A Review of a Review'. Professor Solow responded with 'A Rejoinder'. Another friendly critic was Professor J. E. Meade – ED.]
15   Octagon, New York, 1946 (reprinted 1970).
16   [William Letwin is Professor of Political Science at the London School of Economics. His wife, Shirley Letwin, has taught, *inter alia*, at the LSE and is the author of *The Pursuit of Certainty*, Cambridge University Press, 1965, and other works. – ED.]
17   Cambridge University Press, 1963.
18   [A reference to a deviation from the monetarist view that trade unions have no direct rôle in generating inflation. The deviating view is that unions in strong bargaining positions can in Britain induce government to inflate in

order to stimulate demand and so avoid the unemployment that would follow monopoly labour costs that cannot be passed on in higher prices. The process is not 'cost-push', but 'politician-push'; the mechanism or instrument of inflation remains the money supply, mismanaged by government monopoly. – ED.]

19   [The BBC interviewer; he is the producer of the BBC radio programme 'Dateline'. – ED.]

20   *Newsweek*, 12 April 1976.

21   [The term 'reverse income tax' was coined in IEA writings: *Policy for Poverty*, Research Monograph 20, 1970; *Choice in Welfare, 1970*, 1971; and others. The reason was simply that, if a tax was a payment to the fisc, a tax in reverse was a payment from the fisc. – ED.]

22   Daniel P. Moynihan, *The Politics of a Guaranteed Income*, Random House, New York, 1973.

23   [The proposal for an education voucher in the UK, and the moves to an experiment by Kent County Council (*Education Vouchers in Kent: A Feasibility Study for the Education Department*, Kent County Council, 1978), are being opposed mainly by the educational bureaucracy in the National Union of Teachers and elsewhere, or rather by the spokesmen for teachers. The voucher idea also met resistance in the Layfield Committee (*Local Government Finance: Report of the Committee of Enquiry*, Cmnd. 6453, HMSO, 1976): Ralph Harris and Arthur Seldon, *Pricing or Taxing?: Evidence to the Layfield Committee and a Critique of its Report*, Hobart Paper 71, IEA, 1976. – ED.]

24   David Friedman, Assistant Professor of Economics, Virginia Polytechnic Institute, Blacksburg, Virginia.

25   [*The Vote Motive* is the title of a Hobart Paperback (No. 9) by Professor Gordon Tullock and Dr Morris Perlman, IEA, 1976. – ED.]

26   [This is a reference to the diverse sectional resistances to the 1944 Education Bill. 'We decided at the very outset to make the [educational] reform as comprehensive as possible, and if there were any nettles to get a good bunch of them in our arms and not be stung by a little one. That policy has proved extremely successful ... because the more nettles you collect the more they sting one another and the less they sting you.' Quoted from Ralph Harris, *Politics without Prejudice*, Staples Press, London, 1956. – ED.]

8

Roofs or Ceilings?: the Current Housing Problem *with George J. Stigler*

1 The Background

The San Francisco earthquake of 18 April 1906, was followed by great fires which in three days utterly destroyed 3,400 acres of buildings in the heart of the city.

Major General Greely, commander of the Federal troops in the area, described the situation in these terms:

> Not a hotel of note or importance was left standing. The great apartment houses had vanished ... Two hundred and twenty-five thousand people were ... homeless.

In addition, the earthquake damaged or destroyed many other homes. Thus a city of about 400,000 lost more than half of its housing facilities in three days.

Various factors mitigated the acute shortage of housing. Many people temporarily left the city – one estimate is as high as 75,000. Temporary camps and shelters were established and at their peak, in the summer of 1906, cared for about 30,000 people. New construction proceeded rapidly.

However, after the disaster, it was necessary for many months for perhaps one-fifth of the city's former population to be absorbed into the remaining half of the housing facilities. In other words, each remaining house on average had to shelter 40 per cent more people.

Yet when one turns to the *San Francisco Chronicle* of 24 May 1906 –

(1972) (a revised version of a paper first published in *Popular Essays on Current Problems*, Vol. 1, No. 2, September 1946).

the first available issue after the earthquake – *there is not a single mention of a housing shortage!* The classified advertisements listed 64 offers (some for more than one dwelling) of flats and houses for rent, and 19 of houses for sale, against five advertisements of flats or houses wanted. Then and thereafter a considerable number of all types of accommodation except hotel rooms were offered for rent.

Rationing by rents or chance?

Forty years later another housing shortage descended on San Francisco. This time the shortage was nation-wide. The situation in San Francisco was not the worst in the nation, but because of the migration westward it was worse than average. In 1940, the population of 635,000 had no shortage of housing, in the sense that only 93 per cent of the dwelling units were occupied. By 1946 the population had increased by at most a third – about 200,000. Meanwhile the number of dwelling units had increased by at least a fifth.

Therefore, the city was being asked to shelter 10 per cent more people in each dwelling-unit than before the war. One might say that the shortage in 1946 was one-quarter as acute as in 1906, when each remaining dwelling-unit had to shelter 40 per cent more people than before the earthquake.

In 1946, however, the housing shortage did not pass unnoticed by the *Chronicle* or by others. On 8 January the California state legislature was convened and the Governor listed the housing shortage as 'the most critical problem facing California'. During the first five days of the year there were altogether only four advertisements offering houses or apartments for rent, as compared with 64 in one day in May 1906, and nine advertisements offering to exchange quarters in San Francisco for quarters elsewhere. But in 1946 there were 30 advertisements per day by persons wanting to rent houses or apartments, against only five in 1906 after the great disaster. During this same period in 1946, there were about 60 advertisements per day of houses for sale, as against 19 in 1906.

In both 1906 and 1946, San Francisco was faced with the problem that now confronts the entire nation: how can a relatively fixed amount of housing be divided (that is, rationed) among people who wish much more until new construction can fill the gap? In 1906 the rationing was done by higher rents. In 1946, the use of higher rents to ration housing has been made illegal by the imposition of rent ceilings, and the rationing is by chance and favouritism. A third possibility would be for OPA to undertake the rationing.

What are the comparative merits of these three methods?

2 The 1906 Method: Price Rationing

War experience has led many people to think of rationing as equivalent to OPA forms, coupons, and orders.

But this is a superficial view; everything that is not as abundant as air or sunlight must, in a sense, be rationed. That is, whenever people want more of something than can be had for the asking, whether bread, theatre tickets, blankets, or haircuts, there must be some way of determining how it shall be distributed among those who want it.

Our normal peace-time basis of rationing has been the method of the auction sale. If demand for anything increases, competition among buyers tends to raise its price. The rise in price causes buyers to use the article more sparingly, carefully, and economically, and thereby reduces consumption to the supply. At the same time, the rise in price encourages producers to expand output. Similarly, if the demand for any article decreases, the price tends to fall, expanding consumption to the supply and discouraging output.

In 1906 San Francisco used this free-market method to deal with its housing problems, with a consequent rise of rents. Yet, although rents were higher than before the earthquake, it is cruel to present-day house seekers to quote a 1906 post-disaster advertisement: 'Six-room house and bath, with 2 additional rooms in basement having fire-places, nicely furnished; fine piano; ... $45'.

The advantages of rationing by higher rents are clear from our example:

1 In a free market, there is always some housing immediately available for rent – at all rent levels.
2 The bidding up of rents forces some people to economise on space. *Until there is sufficient new construction, this doubling up is the only solution.*
3 The high rents act as a strong stimulus to new construction.
4 No complex, expensive, and expansive machinery is necessary. The rationing is conducted quietly and impersonally through the price system.

The full significance of these advantages will be clearer when we have considered the alternatives.

Objections to price rationing

Against these merits, which before the war were scarcely questioned in the United States, three offsetting objections are now raised.

(a) The first objection is usually stated in this form: 'The rich will get all the housing, and the poor none.'

This objection is false: *At all times during the acute shortage in 1906 inexpensive flats and houses were available.* What is true is that, under free-market conditions, the better quarters will go to those who pay more, either because they have larger incomes or more wealth, or because they prefer housing to, say, better automobiles.

But this fact has no more relation to the housing problem of today than to that of 1940. In fact, if inequality of income and wealth among individuals justifies rent controls now, it provided an even stronger reason for such controls in 1940. The danger, if any, that the rich would get all the housing was even greater then than now.

Each person or family is now using at least as much housing space, on the average, as before the war (below, p. 179). Furthermore, the total income of the nation is now distributed more equally among the nation's families than before the war. Therefore, *if rents were freed from legal control and left to seek their own levels, as much housing as was occupied before the war would be distributed more equally than it was then.*

That better quarters go under free-market conditions to those who have larger incomes or more wealth is, if anything, simply a reason for taking long-term measures to reduce the inequality of income and wealth. For those, like us, who would like even more equality than there is at present, not just for housing but for all products, it is surely better to attack directly existing inequalities in income and wealth at their source than to ration each of the hundreds of commodities and services that compose our standard of living. It is the height of folly to permit individuals to receive unequal money-incomes and then to take elaborate and costly measures to prevent them from using their incomes.

(b) The second objection often raised to removing rent controls is that landlords would benefit. Rents would certainly rise, except in the so-called black market; and so would the incomes of landlords. But is this an objection? Some groups will gain under any system of rationing, and it is certainly true that urban residential landlords have benefited less than almost any other large group from the war expansion.

The ultimate solution of the housing shortage must come through new construction. Much of this new construction will be for owner-occupancy. But many persons prefer to or must live in rented properties. Increase or improvement of housing for such persons depends in large part on the construction of new properties to rent. It is an odd way to encourage new rental construction (that is, becoming a landlord) by grudging enterprising builders an attractive return.

(c) The third current objection to a free market in housing is that a rise in rents means an inflation, or leads to one.

But price inflation is a rise of many individual prices, and it is much simpler to attack the threat at its source, which is the increased family income and liquid resources that finance the increased spending on almost everything. Heavy taxation,[1] governmental economies, and control of the stock of money are the fundamental weapons to fight inflation. Tinkering with millions of individual prices – the rent of house A in San Francisco, the price of steak B in Chicago, the price of suit C in New York – means dealing clumsily and ineffectively with the symptoms and results of inflation instead of its real causes.

Yet, it will be said, we are not invoking fiscal and monetary controls, and are not likely to do so, so the removal of rent ceilings *will*, in practice, incite wage and then price increases – the familiar inflationary spiral. We do not dispute that this position is tenable, but is it convincing? To answer, we must, on the one hand, appraise the costs of continued rent control, and, on the other, the probable additional contribution to inflation from a removal of rent controls. We shall discuss the costs of the present system next, and in the conclusion briefly appraise the inflationary threat of higher rents.

The present rationing of houses for sale

The absence of a ceiling on the selling price of housing means that at present homes occupied by their owners are being rationed by the 1906 method – to the highest bidder. The selling price of houses is rising as the large and increasing demand encounters the relatively fixed supply. Consequently, many a landlord is deciding that it is better to sell at the inflated market price than to rent at a fixed ceiling price.

The ceiling on rents, therefore, means that an increasing fraction of all housing is being put on the market for owner-occupation, and that rentals are becoming almost impossible to find, at least at the legal rents. In 1906, when both rents and selling prices were free to rise, the *San Francisco Chronicle* listed three 'houses for sale' for every 10 'houses or apartments for rent'. In 1946, under rent control, about 730 'houses for sale' were listed for every 10 'houses or apartments for rent'.

The free market in houses for sale therefore permits a man who has enough capital to make the down-payment on a house to solve his problem by purchase. Often this means that he must go heavily into debt, and that he puts into the down-payment what he would have preferred to spend in other ways.

Nevertheless, the man who has money will find plenty of houses – and attractive ones at that – to buy. The prices will be high – but that is the reason houses are available. He is likely to end up with less desirable housing, furnishings, and other things than he would like, or than his memories of pre-war prices had led him to hope he might get, but at least he will have a roof over his family.

The methods of rent control used in 1946, therefore, do not avoid one of the chief criticisms directed against rationing by higher rents – that the rich have an advantage in satisfying their housing needs. Indeed, the 1946 methods make this condition worse. By encouraging existing renters to use space freely and compelling many to borrow and buy who would prefer to rent, present methods make the price rise in houses-for-sale larger than it would be if there were no rent controls.

One way to avoid giving persons with capital first claim to an increasing share of housing would be to impose a ceiling on the selling price of houses. This would reduce still further the area of price rationing and correspondingly extend present rent-control methods of rationing rental property. This might be a wise move *if* the present method of rationing rented dwellings were satisfactory.

But what is the situation of the man who wishes to rent?

3 The 1946 Method: Rationing by Chance and Favouritism

The prospective renter is in a position very different from that of the man who is willing to buy. If he can find accommodation, he may pay a 'reasonable', that is, pre-war rent. But unless he is willing to pay a considerable sum on the side – for 'furniture' or in some other devious manner – he is not likely to find anything to rent.

The legal ceilings on rents are the reason why there are so few places for rent. National money-income has doubled, so that most individuals and families are receiving far higher money-incomes than before the war. They are thus able to pay substantially higher rents than before the war, yet legally they need pay no more; they are therefore trying to get more and better housing.

But not all the millions of persons and families who have thus been trying to spread out since 1940 can succeed, since the supply of housing has increased only about as fast as population. Those who do succeed force others to go without housing. The attempt by the less fortunate and the newcomers to the housing market – returning service men, newly-weds, and people changing homes – to get more housing space than is available and more than they used before the war, leads to the familiar spectacle of a horde of applicants for each vacancy.

Advertisements in the *San Francisco Chronicle* again document the effect of rent ceilings. In 1906, after the earthquake, when rents were free to rise, there was one 'wanted for rent' for every 10 'houses or apartments for rent'; in 1946, there were 375 'wanted for rent' for every 10 'for rent'.

A 'veteran' looks for a house

The *New York Times* for 28 January 1946 reported the experience of Charles Schwartzman, 'a brisk young man in his early thirties', recently released from the army. Mr Schwartzman hunted strenuously for three months,

> ... riding around in his car looking for a place to live ... He had covered the city and its environs from Jamaica, Queens, to Larchmont and had registered with virtually every real estate agency. He had advertised in the newspapers and he had answered advertisements. He had visited the New York City Veterans Center at 500 Park Avenue and the American Veterans Committee housing sub-committee; he had spoken to friends, he had pleaded with relatives; he had written to Governor Dewey. The results?
> An offer of a sub-standard cold-water flat. An offer of four rooms at Central Park West and 101st Street at a rental of $300 a month provided he was prepared to pay $5,000 for the furniture in the apartment. An offer of one room in an old brownstone house, repainted but not renovated, at Eighty-eighth Street off Central Park West by a young woman (who was going to Havana) at a rental of $80 a month, provided he buy the furniture

for $1,300 and reimburse her for the $100 she had to pay an agent to obtain the 'apartment'.

And a sub-let offer of two commodious rooms in a West Side hotel at a rental of $75 a month only to find that the hotel owner had taken the suite off the monthly rental list and placed it on the transient list with daily (and higher) rates for each of the rooms.

Who gets the housing?

Rental property is now rationed by various forms of chance and favouritism. First priority goes to the family that rented before the housing shortage and is willing to remain in the same dwelling.

Second priority goes to two classes among recent arrivals: (i) persons willing and able to avoid or evade[2] rent ceilings, either by some legal device or by paying a cash supplement to the OPA ceiling rent; (ii) friends or relatives of landlords or other persons in charge of renting dwellings.

Prospective tenants not in these favoured classes scramble for any remaining places. Success goes to those who are lucky, have the smallest families, can spend the most time in hunting, are most ingenious in devising schemes to find out about possible vacancies, and are the most desirable tenants.

Last priority is likely to go to the man who must work to support his family and whose wife must care for small children. He and his wife can spend little time looking for the needle in the haystack. And if he should find a place, it may well be refused him because a family with small children is a less desirable tenant than a childless family.

Socio-economic costs of present methods

Practically everyone who does not succeed in buying a house or renting a house or apartment is housed somehow. A few are housed in emergency dwellings – trailer camps, prefabricated emergency housing units, reconverted army camps. Most are housed by doubling-up with relatives or friends, a solution that has serious social disadvantages.

The location of relatives or friends willing and able to provide housing may bear little or no relation to the desired location. In order to live with his family, the husband must sacrifice mobility and take whatever position is available in the locality. If no position or only an inferior one is available there, he may have to separate himself from his family for an unpredictable period to take advantage of job opportunities elsewhere. Yet there is a great social need for mobility (especially at present). The best distribution of population after the war certainly differs from the war-time distribution, and rapid reconversion requires that men be willing and able to change their location.

The spectre of current methods of doubling-up restricts the movement not only of those who double up but also of those who do not. The man who is fortunate enough to have a house or apartment will think twice before moving to another city where he will be one of the disfavoured recent arrivals. One of the most easily predictable costs of moving is likely to be an extended separation from his family while he hunts for housing and they stay where they are or move in on relatives.

The rent ceilings also have important effects in reducing the efficiency with which housing is now being used by those who do not double up. The incentives to economise space are much weaker than before the war, because rents are now lower relatively to average money-incomes. If it did not seem desirable to move to smaller quarters before the war, or to take in a lodger, there is no added reason to do so now, except patriotic and humanitarian impulses – or possibly the fear of relatives descending on the extra space!

Indeed, the scarcity resulting from rent ceilings imposes new impediments to the efficient use of housing: a tenant will not often abandon his overly-large apartment to begin the dreary search for more appropriate quarters. And every time a vacancy does occur the landlord is likely to give preference in renting to smaller families or the single.

The removal of rent ceilings would bring about doubling up in an entirely different manner. In a free rental market those people would yield up space who considered the sacrifice of space repaid by the rent received. Doubling-up would be by those who had space to spare and wanted extra income, not, as now, by those who act from a sense of family duty or obligation, regardless of space available or other circumstances. Those who rented space from others would be engaging in a strictly business transaction, and would not feel that they were intruding, accumulating personal obligations, or imposing unfair or unwelcome burdens on benefactors. They would be better able to find rentals in places related to their job opportunities. Workers would regain their mobility and owners of rental properties their incentive to take in more persons.

4 The Method of Public Rationing

The defects in our present method of rationing by landlords are obvious and weighty. They are to be expected under private personal rationing, which is, of course, why OPA assumed the task of rationing meats, fats, canned goods, and sugar during the war instead of letting grocers ration them. Should OPA undertake the task of rationing housing? Those who advocate the rationing of housing by a public agency argue that this would eliminate the discrimination against new arrivals, against families with children, and in favour of families with well-placed friends.

Problems of 'political' rationing

To be fair between owners and renters, however, OPA would have to be able to tell owners that they had excessive space and must either yield up a portion or shift to smaller quarters. One's ear need not be close to the ground to know that it is utterly impracticable from a political viewpoint to order an American family owning its home either to take in a strange family (for free choice would defeat the purpose of rationing) or to move out.

Even if this basic difficulty were surmountable, how could the amount of space that a particular family deserves be determined? At what age do children of different sex require separate rooms? Do invalids need ground-floor dwellings, and who is an invalid? Do persons who work in their own homes (physicians, writers, musicians) require more space? What occupations should be favoured by handy locations, and what families by large gardens? Must a mother-in-law live with the family, or is she entitled to a separate dwelling?

How long would it take an OPA board to answer these questions and to decide what tenants or owners must 'move over' to make room for those who, in the board's opinion, should have it?

The duration of the housing shortage would also be affected. In fairness to both tenants and existing landlords, new construction would also have to be rationed and subjected to rent control. If rents on new dwellings were set considerably higher than on comparable existing dwellings, in order to stimulate new construction, one of the main objectives of rent control and rationing – equal treatment for all – would be sacrificed. On the other hand, if rents on new dwellings were kept the same as rents on existing dwellings, private construction of properties for rent would be small or non-existent.

We may conclude that rationing by a public agency is unlikely to be accepted on a thorough-going basis. Even if applied only to rented dwellings, it would raise stupendous administrative and ethical problems.

Sources and probable duration of the present shortage

The present housing shortage appears so acute, in the light of the moderate increase in population and the real increase in housing since 1940, that most people are at a loss for a general explanation. Rather they refer to the rapid growth of some cities – but all cities have serious shortages. Or they refer to the rise in marriage and birth rates – but these numbers are rarely measured, or compared with housing facilities.

Actually, the supply of housing has about kept pace with the growth of civilian non-farm population, as the estimates based on government data show (table 1). Certain areas will be more crowded in a physical sense than in 1940, and others less crowded, but the broad fact stands out that the number of people to be housed and the number of families have increased by about 10 per cent, and the number of dwelling-units has also increased by about 10 per cent.

Table 1   *Rise in housing and non-farm population, USA, 1940–6*

	Non-farm		
	Occupied dwelling-units (million)	Civilian population (million)	Persons per occupied dwelling-unit (no.)
30 June 1940	27.9	101	3.6
30 June 1944	30.6	101	3.3
End of Demobilisation (spring 1946)	More than 31.3	About 111	Less than 3.6

Two factors explain why the housing shortage seems so much more desperate now than in 1940, even though the amount of housing per person or family is about the same.

1   The aggregate money-income of the American public has doubled since 1940, so that the average family could afford larger and better living-quarters even if rents had risen substantially.

2   Rents have risen very little. They rose by less than 4 per cent from June 1940 to September 1945, while all other items in the cost of living rose by 33 per cent.

Thus, both the price structure and the increase in income encourage the average family to secure better living quarters than before the war. *The very success of OPA in regulating rents has therefore contributed largely to the demand for housing and hence to the shortage, for housing is cheap relatively to other things.*

Future housing problems

Rent ceilings do nothing to alleviate this shortage. Indeed, they are far more likely to perpetuate it: the implications of the rent ceilings for new construction are ominous. Rent is the only important item in the cost of living that has not risen rapidly. Unless there is a violent deflation, which no-one wants and no administration can permit, rents are out of line with all other significant prices and costs, including building costs. New construction must therefore be disappointingly small in volume *unless* (1) an industrial revolution reduces building costs dramatically, or (2) the government subsidises the construction industry.

The industrial revolution in building methods is devoutly to be wished. But if it comes, it will come much faster if rents are higher. If it does not come, existing construction methods will, for the most part, deliver houses only to those who can afford and wish to own their homes. Homes to rent will become harder and harder to find.

Subsidies for building, in the midst of our high money-incomes and urgent demand for housing, would be an unnecessary paradox. Now, if ever, people are able to pay for their housing. If subsidies were successful in stimulating building, rent ceilings could gradually be removed without a rise in rents. But building costs would still be high (higher than if there had been no subsidy) and so housing construction would slump to low levels and remain there for a long period. Gradually, the supply of housing would fall and the population rise sufficiently to raise rents to remunerative levels. A subsidy thus promises a depression of unprecedented severity in residential construction; it would be irresponsible optimism to hope for a prosperous economy when this great industry was sick.

Unless, therefore, we are lucky (a revolutionary reduction in the cost of building apartments and houses), or unlucky (a violent deflation), or especially unwise (the use of subsidies), the 'housing shortage' will remain as long as rents are held down by legal controls. *As long as the shortage created by rent ceilings remains, there will be a clamour for continued rent controls.* This is perhaps the strongest indictment of ceilings on rents. They, and the accompanying shortage of dwellings to rent, perpetuate themselves, and the progeny are even less attractive than the parents.

An incomplete and largely subconscious realisation of this uncomfortable dilemma explains the frequent proposal that no rent ceilings or that more generous ceilings be imposed on new construction. This proposal involves a partial abandonment of rent ceilings. The retention of the rest can then be defended only on the ground that the present method of rationing existing housing by chance and favouritism is more equitable than rationing by higher rents, but that rationing the future supply of housing by higher rents is more equitable than rationing by present methods.

5 Conclusions

Rent ceilings, therefore, cause haphazard and arbitrary allocation of space, inefficient use of space, retardation of new construction and indefinite continuance of rent ceilings, or subsidisation of new construction and a future depression in residential building. Formal rationing by public authority would probably make matters worse.

Unless removal of rent ceilings would be a powerful new stimulus to inflation, therefore, there is no important defence for them. In practice, higher rents would have little *direct* inflationary pressure on other goods and services. The extra income received by landlords would be offset by the decrease in the funds available to tenants for the purchase of other goods and services.

The additional inflationary pressure from higher rents would arise *indirectly*; the higher rents would raise the cost of living and thereby provide an excuse for wage rises. In an era of direct governmental intervention in wage-fixing, the existence of this excuse might lead to some wage rises that would not otherwise occur and therefore to some further price rises.

How important would this indirect effect be? Immediately after the removal of ceilings, rents charged to new tenants and some existing tenants without leases would rise substantially. Most existing tenants would experience moderate rises, or, if protected by leases, none at all. Since dwellings enter the rental market only slowly, average rents on all dwellings would rise far less than rents charged to new tenants and the cost of living would rise even less.

As more dwellings entered the rental market, the initial rise in rents charged to new tenants would, in the absence of general inflation, be moderated, although average rents on all dwellings would continue to rise.

After a year or so, average rents might be up by as much as 30 per cent. But even this would mean a rise of only about 5 per cent in the cost of living, since rents account for less than one-fifth of the cost of living. A rise of this magnitude – less than one-half of 1 per cent per month in the cost of living – is hardly likely to start a general inflation.

The problem of preventing general inflation should be attacked directly; it cannot be solved by special controls in special areas which may for a time bottle up the basic inflationary pressures but do not remove them. We do not believe, therefore, that rent ceilings are a sufficient defence against inflation to merit even a fraction of the huge social costs they entail.

No solution of the housing problem can benefit everyone; some must be hurt. The essence of the problem is that some people must be compelled or induced to use less housing than they are willing to pay for at present legal rents. Existing methods of rationing housing are forcing a small minority – primarily released veterans and migrating war workers, along with their families, friends and relatives – to bear the chief sacrifice.

Rationing by higher rents would aid this group by inducing many others to use less housing and would, therefore, have the merit of spreading the burden more evenly among the population as a whole. It would hurt more people immediately, *but less severely*, than the existing methods. This is, at one and the same time, the justification for using high rents to ration housing and the chief political obstacle to the removal of rent ceilings.

A final note to the reader: we should like to emphasise as strongly as possible that our objectives are the same as yours – *the most equitable possible distribution of the available supply of housing* and *the speediest possible resumption of new construction*. The rise in rents that would follow the removal of rent control is not a virtue in itself. We have no desire to pay higher rents, to see others forced to pay them, or to see landlords reap windfall profits. Yet we urge the removal of rent ceilings because, in our view, any other solution of the housing problem involves still worse evils.

Notes

1 [This may have been true in the USA of 1946. There is increasing doubt whether it is true in the Britain of 1972 if high taxes reduce 'take-home' pay and encourage strong trade unions to demand large increases that monetary expansion enables employers to grant. – ED.]
2 [These words have the same meaning as in Britain: tax evasion is the illegal concealment of taxable earnings, tax avoidance is the legitimate reduction of taxable income to the minimum. – ED.]

Index